D1146366

America's Work Force is Coming of Age

"This book is must reading in this time of diminishing numbers of young workers and the need of seniors for post-retirement activity. I cannot think of any phase of the subject that has not been treated in this analysis of the problems, challenges, and opportunities for older people to join the American work force."

—Art Linkletter

"Because of the shortage of qualified people in the labor market, employers will have to rethink present retirement policies and develop policies to retain and attract the older work force. *America's Work Force is Coming of Age* is a comprehensive approach to dealing with the needs of the older work force and provides practical, how-to information about utilizing this important national asset. An information gap exists in dealing with the recruitment, retention, and management of older workers. This book is an invaluable guide in closing that gap."

—Irene Adams
Senior Vice President
Kelly Services, Inc.

"Managing an aging work force will become a challenge faced by all businesses. Reading this book will raise your level of awareness on how to best cope with the challenge."

—Anne Blouin, C.A.E.
Manager of Education
American Society of Association Executives

"Cathy Fyock has found a way to teach new tricks to a business community that can't afford to keep old ideas. *America's Work Force is Coming of Age* contains a thorough overview of the rethinking we must do in order to tap a valuable labor pool."

—Paul Austermuehle
Vice President, Recruitment Advertising Division
Bentley, Barnes, & Lynn Advertising

"Our nation cannot avoid turning to older adults to meet its labor-force needs. This is the first book to spell out what businesses can do to attract and retain the older worker successfully. *America's Work Force is Coming of Age* is excellent."

—Jeanette Takaamura, Ph.D.
Director, Executive Office on Aging
Hawaii

America's Work Force is Coming of Age

What Every Business Needs to
Know to Recruit, Train, Manage,
and Retain an Aging Work Force

Catherine D. Fyock, A.E.P.

Lexington Books

D.C. Heath and Company/Lexington, Massachusetts/Toronto

Library of Congress Cataloging-in-Publication Data

Fyock, Catherine D.
    America's work force is coming of age : what every business needs
to know to recruit, train, manage, and retain an aging work force /
Catherine D. Fyock.
        p.   cm.
    ISBN 0-669-21884-7 (alk. paper)
    1. Aged--Employment--United States.   2. Personnel management-
-United States.   I. Title.
HF5549.5.O44F96   1990
658.3'042--dc20
                                                                90-35971
                                                                CIP

Published simultaneously in Canada
Printed in the United States of America
Casebound International Standard Book Number: 0-669-21884-7
Library of Congress Catalog Card Number: 90-35971

The paper used in this publication meets the minimum requirements of
American National Standard for Information Sciences—Permanence of
Paper for Printed Library Materials, ANSI Z39.48-1984. ∞ ™

Year and number of this printing:

90 91 92 8 7 6 5 4 3 2 1

To my husband, Jim, who gave me constant support and encouragement for this book; To my mother, an older worker who gave me inspiration for life.

Contents

Tables and Figures   xi

Introduction   xiii

1. Coming of Age: The Older Worker as a Staffing
   Solution   1

   The Graying of America . . . and the World   3
   Baby Boomers Grow Up   4
   Life Expectancy on the Rise   5
   *Labor Force Participation Declines for Older
   Workers   6*
   The Baby Bust as a Reality   7
   Labor Shortages Abound   9
   "Ain't It Awful?"   10
   Labor Costs on the Rise   12
   Skills in Demand Lack Young Workers   13
   Changing Perceptions about Older Americans   14
   Reaching the Older Customer Is Big Business   15
   Businesses' Response to the Aging Workplace   20

2. The New Older Worker: A Profile   29

   Myths and Realities   31
   Demographics   41
   Occupations   46
   Perceptions of Work   46
   The Diversity of Older People   49

3. Hiring Experience: Attracting and Selecting Older Workers 57

New Staffing Principles 57
Recruiting Older Workers 61
Selecting Older Workers 91

4. Teaching New Tricks: Training and Retraining the Older Worker 97

Orienting the New Older Worker to the Job 99
Pretraining 100
Adult Learning Principles Revisited 101
Differences in Learning 103
Adapting the Training Process 105
Instructors Need New Methodologies 106
Teaching High-technology Skills 109
Assessing the Older Worker 111
Challenges of Career Development 115
Supervisory Training: Managing a Diverse Work Force 118
Training Support Available to Employers 120
Preretirement Training 120
Summary 120

5. Dollars and Sense: Compensation Issues and the Older Worker 123

Salary: How Much to Pay? 124
Pay and Social Security Benefits 125
Importance of Benefits 128
Cost Containment and Wellness Programs 129
Eldercare and Long-term Care 132
Pensions 137
Postretirement Medical Benefits 140
Medicare 140
Social Security 142
Summary 143

6. Valuing Experience: Managing and Retaining an Aging Work Force 147

Barriers in Managing and Retaining Older Workers 148
Values and Work Ethics 150
Flexible Work Schedules 154
Job Redesign 168
Career Management and Development 170
Age Discrimination and Ageism 176
Managing for Retention of Older Workers 184
Summary 185

7. Retirement and the Aging Work Force 189

Why the Early Retirement Trend? 190
Planning for Retirement 191
Planning and Implementing a Preretirement Program 197
Summary 200

8. Putting Experience to Work: Models in Employing Older Workers 201

Corporate Solutions: Putting Experience to Work 202
Redesigning Work for the Aging Work Force 204
Services to Assist in the Employment of Older Workers 206
Making It Work: Putting Experience Back to Work 208
Brainpower and Talent 215

Appendix 219
Index 243
About the Author 249

Tables and Figures

Tables

2–1. Incentives That Might Keep a Person at Work Past Retirement Age   49

5–1. Social Security Earnings Guidelines   127

5–2. Potential Earnings Chart   128

6–1. Differences in Values for "Traditionalists" and "Challengers"   152

Figures

1–1. Average Age of America's Workers   2

1–2. Baby Boomers and Baby Busters   8

2–1. Work Force Participation Rates   43

3–1. Focus on Esteem Need   62

3–2. Focus on Security Need   63

3–3. Focus on Financial Need   64

3–4. Focus on Social Need   65

Introduction

Each year as I grow older I become more aware of the "Graying of America," as well as my place in the aging work force.

The environment is improving for older workers, but it still is not at the point I would like for it to be when I get there. Age discrimination, ageist language, stereotyping, and persistent myths about the aging worker still exist. My goal is that when I "arrive," I will be able to work at my optimum potential, doing what I want to do, where I want, when I want. I don't want to be placed into an arbitrary pigeonhole determined by someone's stereotype of me. I believe we all want the opportunity to age gracefully and productively.

One of my motivations for writing this book is to ensure that I have a safe place in tomorrow's work force. Yet I do have another motivation—one that is a bit selfish. My mother is considered to be an "older worker," but if you knew her you would see she is enthusiastic and vibrant. She is energetic and open to new ideas. At the age of fifty-five, she decided having her bachelor's degree was important to her, so she quit her job and returned to school full time, despite protests from family and friends who said, "You have a good job and you may not get back into the work force if you quit now." She has since been awarded her bachelor's degree in psychology, and has gone on to earn her master's in vocational counseling. Now she is looking for something just right for her, while working for me part time.

When I think about her vitality and all she has to offer the workplace, I want employers to realize that they waste a valuable resource when they overlook her because of her age. I want organizations to understand that they do a terrible injustice—to themselves and to all older workers—when they perpetuate stereotypes and discriminatory practices. I want my mother's potential to be realized, and I want this human resource to be valued and cherished.

I wrote this book for individuals who cannot find work because of their age, for those who are forced into "early retirement," and for those who are underemployed in jobs they don't want because employers fail to see their value.

I also wrote this book for those of you in corporations who are genuinely interested in tapping into this resource. When I was with Kentucky Fried Chicken Corporation, we became interested in doing a better job of attracting older workers for all positions in the company (not just entry-level positions). We created a national initiative for attracting and retaining older workers, which we called "The Colonel's Tradition"—named after the Colonel, Harland Sanders, who began the company when he was sixty-five years old.

The problem I encountered when beginning was that employer-centered information was scarce. Most publications at that time were written by gerontologists, and not necessarily those with an employer's perspective. I found some information here and there, but no one resource really captured the issues in employing older workers that were important to the human resource manager or business owner. And so I recognized my mission: to create a resource for business people, written by a business person, to capture the essential issues in employing the experienced worker.

This book provides you with practical, workable information on the multiple aspects of managing an aging work force. It gives you hands-on, how-to information based upon my experiences as a human resources manager and as a consultant who has helped businesses find success with older workers as a critical human resource strategy.

The book explores reasons why employing older workers is a smart business decision and why you should be taking action today. It covers demographic information and specifics on all functional areas of employment: recruitment, selection, training, compensation, management, retention, and retirement. It offers case studies and models of employment important for those of you who want to replicate such models in your companies.

This book is intended to be an easy reference guide; each chapter encompasses a different functional area. I hope it becomes the "textbook" for employers who intend to recruit and retain one of their most valuable assets— their older workers.

I also hope that as you read, you will see we all have a lot to gain, directly and indirectly, by opening the workplace for experienced workers. Because you aren't getting any younger, either!

1
Coming of Age: The Older Worker as a Staffing Solution

If you take all the experience and judgment of men over fifty out of
the world, there wouldn't be enough left to run it.
            —Henry Ford

America's workforce not only is growing up, but it also
is getting a few gray hairs! •The average age of the
American worker is increasing, reaching thirty-nine years
by the year 2000, as compared with thirty-one in 1982 and
twenty-nine in 1976.[1]• This is displayed in figure 1–1.
Within the next twenty-five years, 25 percent of the work
force—or one in four workers—will be fifty-five years of
age or older.

Indeed, America's workforce is coming of age, and businesses will need to ready themselves and the work environment to make the most of this radical change and
opportunity.

Today's employers are faced with many new challenges:
an aging work force, a smaller work force with fewer new
entrants, labor shortages in many industries and occupations, increased labor costs, diminished skill levels of an
increasingly uneducated and illiterate work force, and
changing worker values. In many cases, the older worker is
not so much a *problem*, but rather, a *solution* to varied
and complex challenges facing America's businesses.

Many corporations have already seen the advantages of
jumping on the "gray" bandwagon. The Travelers, Wells
Fargo Bank, the Grumman Corp., McDonalds, and many

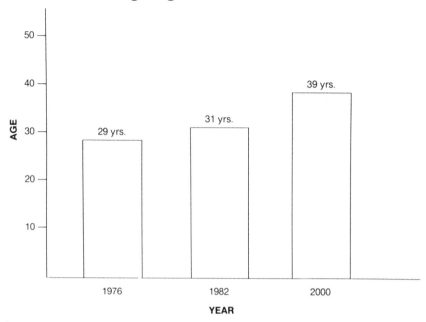

Source: Adapted from "Planning Today for the Future's Changing Shape," by Martha I. Finney in *Personnel Administrator*, January 1989, p. 44.

Figure 1–1.   *Average Age of America's Workers*

others have recognized that the older worker has much to offer in terms of solutions to business issues and concerns. Older workers offer experience, maturity, stability, and wisdom to the workplace, and are increasingly sought after to solve the problems of uneducated, unskilled, and unavailable workers.

What are the forces affecting the work environment of today, and what role will older workers play in redefining work for today and tomorrow? How will mature workers serve as solutions, not as additional problems, for the business leaders of the future? Will older Americans participate in the labor force to meet the demands of increased staffing needs? Will the trend toward early retirement continue, and

---

Forces Affecting America's Business

- The aging work force means more available older workers.
- The baby bust creates labor shortages.
- Increased labor costs affect the bottom line.
- Skills needed by business are not possessed by young workers.
- Many businesses realize the value of older customers.

---

if so, how will it affect worker availability? How will changing perceptions in the marketplace change the complexion of the workplace?

These are questions that face today's business leaders, and there are no easy answers. But increasingly, futurists and others point out that older workers are living longer, more productively, and in much different patterns than in the past. They herald the arrival of an "age wave," as does Ken Dychtwald, author of the recent *Age Wave: The Challenges and Opportunities of an Aging America*. Dychtwald outlines the ways America will change as a result of the increasing numbers of older Americans, as well as the changes that will result in the workplace. Now is the time to prepare!

The Graying of America . . . and the World

America is aging, and so is the world. Global population statistics reveal that from the years 2005 to 2025, the world's population of persons age fifty-five and older will increase versus the younger population, says a recent report published by the U.S. Bureau of the Census titled *An Aging World (An Advance Report) 1987*. The report reveals that the elderly population will reach 410 million by the year 2000. It states that many developing countries will experience dramatic increases in their elderly populations; Mexico, for example, will see a 324 percent increase in its population from 1985 to 2025.[2]

Japan also is experiencing a significant graying process. It now has the longest life expectancy and the fastest-growing number of elderly in the world. Today, 10 percent of its population is older than sixty-five.[3]

Leaders of Japan and the United States have joined forces to discuss this phenomenon at a conference in July 1987. At the conference, sponsored by the Alliance for Aging Research, speakers emphasized that opportunities for "work, productivity and service must not be limited because of age."[4] Indeed, the world will be looking at America as it takes the lead in formulating strategies to productively integrate the older individual into the changing workplace.

Baby Boomers Grow Up

In America, the graying already is taking place. While the most significant graying will occur when the baby boom generation reaches age sixty-five, this will occur after the year 2010. In the meantime, the real age wave will occur as those who are now "thirtysomething"—today's baby boomers—move into middle age.

For business managers, this means the workplace will need to undergo some significant changes in the very near future. As workers grow older and encounter changing needs along life's course, these workers will demand that business respond to their needs. With more dual-career couples and single parents, more flexibility in scheduling and in other work arrangements will be just one of the changes businesses will need to make to retain these workers. Workers in their prime-of-life years will need more benefits, including health, life, eldercare, and retirement plans. Flexible benefit plans will be increasingly important to these workers. Because employees look for stability to meet mortgages and family expenses, companies will need to demonstrate a secure work environment. Middle-agers will prize training and retraining as a means to work their way up the corporate ladder. All in all, this means businesses will need to undergo some major changes just to meet the needs of aging baby boomers in the next few years. Obviously, as boomers age, businesses will need to much more aggressively pursue these workers by means of changes in the work environment.[5]

Life Expectancy on the Rise

With life expectancy increasing, more people are living longer, healthier lives. A recent study by the National Institute on Aging and University of Southern California researchers predicted that the number of Americans over age sixty-five may be as high as 87 million in the next fifty years. Not only does this represent one-fourth of the entire population, but it is also 20 million more than the census projection, and three times the current level. The difference between this study's projected numbers and the census is the difference in assumptions about the death rate. The census assumes there will be no overall decline in the death rate; this study predicts a decline of 2 percent a year.[6]

For businesses, this means that not only is the work force aging, but it is aging more productively. With life expectancy on the rise, many people are retiring at age sixty-five (or earlier) only to find ten, twenty, or thirty years of leisure. It is no wonder that individuals reaching retirement age are now thinking about second or third careers. Businesses' response should include strategies for taking advantage of the tremendous wealth of experience and talent that lies within this group, which is fast becoming too "young" to retire—at least to retire from productive life altogether.

One older woman explains she had looked forward to retirement so that she would have time to do the things she always wanted to do—sewing and gardening. But, she laments, you can only sew so many things or repot so many plants before it becomes boring. A retired man reports a similar story. He had so looked forward to retirement because it meant he could finally spend some real time on his love—golf. However, once he retired and was out golfing every day, it just didn't hold the same appeal. Both these individuals ended up returning to the work force in new and challenging positions, and found that the balance of working and doing the things they really loved made the most sense in their lives.

Businesses will find they can utilize the talents of older workers when they offer them the opportunity to balance outside interests, family commitments, and work. This means schedules will need to be flexible enough to allow this kind of balance.

Labor Force Participation Declines for Older Workers

The labor force participation rate is defined as the ratio of persons in the labor force to the total population sixteen years old and older. While participation rates have always been low for people sixty-five and older, it has continued to decrease since 1950.[7]

As more people have become financially able to retire, and as this practice has become more socially acceptable, more individuals have chosen retirement and early retirement as an option. There has also been the thinking that work is something one must endure until one can afford not to. Conversations among many workers are still about making enough money to retire early. Employers need to work much harder to make the work environment rewarding to retain these skilled and experienced workers.

Workers who are forced into early retirement because of corporate downsizing and other organizational issues are finding that age discrimination is still alive and well in America. The cases of age-bias complaints filed in 1987 numbered twenty-seven thousand—almost twice the number lodged in 1980.[8] Often, older job applicants become discouraged with the disappointments of age discrimination and quit their job search. However, much evidence supports the belief that many of these individuals could be enticed into the workplace if the incentives were right.

It becomes obvious that if businesses are interested in attracting, and more importantly *keeping*, older workers in the workplace, then dramatic changes must occur. Discriminatory practices should be eliminated; more options for retirement and phased retirement need to be examined; more flexible scheduling should be examined. Companies would do well to reconsider eliminating senior workers when going through the downsizing process. It may be that keeping senior workers would be a much better alternative than forcing these workers with skills and experience into early retirement.

The Baby Bust as a Reality

The help-wanted advertisements scream the news; reader-board signs herald "jobs available here"; many entry-level jobs continue to go unfilled. The prospects for continued labor shortages seems to be the wave of the future. Examine the facts:

- There are 72.5 million baby boomers, versus 56.6 million baby busters—those born between 1965 and 1976 (See figure 1–2).

- In 1975 the birthrate sank to 14.6 newborns per 1,000 Americans, the lowest in U.S. history.

- The college-age population has begun to dwindle, with only 27.8 million in 1986, down from 30.1 million in 1983.

- The sixteen- to twenty-four-year-old population has

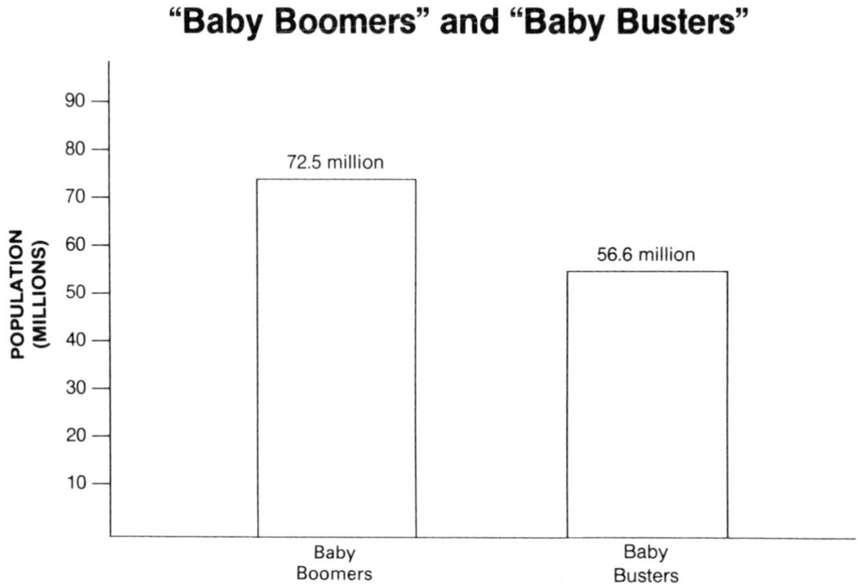

"Baby Boomers" and "Baby Busters"

Source: Adapted from "Welcome, America, to the Baby Bust," by John S. DeMott in *Time*, February 23, 1987, p. 28.

Figure 1–2. *Baby Boomers and Baby Busters*

dropped from 36.5 million in 1975 to 35.3 million in 1986.

- 1992 will graduate the smallest high school class in recent American history.[9]

All these figures spell trouble for businesses, especially those looking to fill entry-level jobs. Consider the headlines:

- "Teen Jobs Go Begging This Summer," in July 1986 *U.S. News and World Report*.
- "Where Are The Teenagers?" in August 1986 *Nation's Business*.
- "For Firms, Any Help Is Hard To find," in July 12, 1988 *USA Today*.
- "Northeast Labor Shortage Forces Retailers To Bend The Rules," in June 1989 *Adweek's Marketing Week*.

Especially in the northeast, where unemployment has been at 3.1 percent (U.S. unemployment for 1988 was 5.5 percent) and has been about 4 percent since 1986, many jobs have gone begging.[10]

Labor Shortages Abound

A special report on labor was issued by the American Society for Personnel Administration (now the Society for Human Resources Management), titled *1988 ASPA Labor Shortage Survey*. In the report, 707 companies were surveyed concerning their perceptions about the labor shortage. At least half the respondents were experiencing moderate or great to very great difficulties in recruiting qualified applicants for all occupational categories listed.[11] This report and others confirm that the shortages are most acute in low-skilled, low-paying jobs (such as waiters, cashiers, hostesses, tellers) and in somewhat better-paying jobs that require higher skills (machinists, nurses, and secretaries). Studies further indicate that while the shortages today remain in these entry-level positions, they will tend to follow the path of the baby busters and will continue into higher-level technical, managerial, and professional occupations and industries.

There is a good news/bad news message for business. The bad news is that the labor shortages are here today for many positions, and will continue to reach all occupations. In other words, if the shortage hasn't hit you yet, it will. The good news, however, is that this shortage is predictable, and can be dealt with intelligently and appropriately by identifying strategies today.

"Ain't It Awful?"

A lament of "ain't it awful?" can be heard from many employers facing labor shortages.

- **"I can't find the quality workers I want—and I don't want to lower my hiring standards."** As businesses become more competitive for the available labor, it becomes increasingly difficult for employers to recruit the cream of the crop.

- **"I can't fill my open positions."** With labor shortages come high vacancy rates, which means many open positions go unfilled. For business this means one person is doing the work of two people, resulting in low morale, burnout, and ultimately, more turnover.

- **"I have high turnover, which adds to my labor costs."** Labor shortages usually mean high turnover, as workers now have many alternatives. High turnover equates with higher recruiting and training costs, affecting the bottom line. Or, worse still, training costs do not go up—meaning that new workers are not being properly trained in the new job. This usually leads to improper preparation for the job, low satisfaction, and in the long run, additional turnover.

- **"I have to pay more to get the people I want."** Labor shortages often lead to higher wages. When companies cannot find the employees they need, wages are increased in hopes of attracting additional workers. The wage wars begin, and wages are driven upward, affecting profitability. Typically, higher starting wages lead to either higher wages at all levels of the organization, or to compression issues as entry-level workers are making wages comparable to those of employees who have been with the organization for some time. Compression inevitably leads to low morale and increased turnover.

- **"I can't open my business without qualified workers."** Labor shortages lead to delayed openings, reduced services, and occasionally, business closings. There have been reports of hospitals throughout the country not being able to open new beds because of inadequate staffing levels of nurses and other health-care professionals. In the northeast, one restaurant chain reported a delayed restaurant opening because the staff could not be recruited in the standard time frame. Some retailers are limiting business hours because of low staffing levels; one fast-food restaurant even closed down the restaurant's dining room and just provided drive-through service during a staffing crunch.

So, while the lament is "ain't it awful?" businesses are understanding that the labor shortage is not only widespread and severe, it is here for a long while. Businesses must discover strategies to deal with fewer entry-level workers to meet growing demands, especially within the growth industries of "high tech" and "high touch"—technology and service industries.

Businesses are beginning to recognize that the older worker is one of the solutions to the labor shortage. Older workers, if attracted to the work force, not only can provide the necessary manpower to solve staffing shortages, but also can serve as quality employees to meet businesses' needs. Employers must learn strategies to aggressively recruit and then retain these workers to meet growing labor demands. Businesses need how-to information, which is outlined in this book.

Labor Costs on the Rise

The shortages of workers, combined with the slower growth rate in the labor force, means labor costs are on the rise. Employers who have traditionally hired younger workers, such as in the retailing and hospitality industries, are already experiencing increased labor costs to recruit and attract these workers. Further, as was discussed earlier, as entry-level wages increase, wages for all workers increase; if not, compression issues arise, coupled with morale problems and higher turnover, which ultimately means higher wages.

As the baby boomers age, they will demand more employee benefits, including more comprehensive health care benefits, long-term care insurance, and aid for caregivers.

Implications for business include the need to be aware of the changing needs of workers and to anticipate those

needs so as to remain competitive in the recruiting wars—
one of the greatest challenges in the upcoming years.

Skills in Demand Lack Young Workers

Today's younger workers often do not have the skills necessary to meet the needs of business. A recent survey from
the departments of Labor, Commerce, and Education reported gaps with younger workers in basic skills such as
writing, math, problem solving, and communication. The
dropout rate in many urban schools is nearing 50 percent.
About 70 million adults are functionally illiterate or borderline illiterate.

And, with a shortage of younger workers from which to
recruit and select, companies are having a harder time in
meeting minimum standards that previously had been expected of job candidates.

If businesses want to select job candidates with skills
and abilities that match job requirements, one approach is
to attract more older workers into the workplace. Typically, older workers, more than their younger counterparts,
possess these basic skills so necessary on the job. This,
coupled with their life experiences and job-relevant knowledge, makes them excellent candidates to reenter the job
market.

The second approach businesses should consider is that
of retaining their older employees already in the workplace.
By keeping older workers, employers can benefit from the
job-specific information learned by these workers throughout their employment. Further, by offering continued on-
the-job training and retraining to these workers, employers
find that their needs for employees with appropriate skill
levels are met.

Consider the example of Shenandoah Life Insurance in

Roanoke, Virginia—a company that plans to keep its employees for life. It intends to live up to this commitment by providing the kind of ongoing training to its workers that permits them to remain productive and satisfied on the job.

In 1978 Shenandoah, along with the entire insurance industry, underwent a tremendous change in processing of claims. Technological advances made it possible to speed up the entire process and heighten productivity. Yet, in an attitude survey, employees revealed low morale and a lack of communication. As a result, Shenandoah initiated a new training program that incorporated quality circles and a pay-for-knowledge program. Now the company boasts a 42.7 percent increase in productivity from 1985 to 1989 as a result of this program, and their employees have a new commitment to the company. One employee said in an interview with *Personnel Administrator*, "I'm doing more than I ever thought I could . . . but I'm at Shenandoah for life . . . or at least as long as they'll have me."[12]

Changing Perceptions about Older Americans

It wasn't that long ago that America thought its older Americans were over the hill. A quick look at greeting cards demonstrated that age was not highly regarded in this country. Some of the messages on greeting cards, coffee mugs, T-shirts, and bumper stickers included:

- "Thirty isn't old if you're a tree."
- "Age and treachery will overcome youth and skill."
- "Pushing forty is exercise enough."
- "I may be getting older, but I refuse to grow up."

Older people were seldom portrayed on television, especially in proportion to the percentage of older people watching. When older people were portrayed, it was the character typical of Aunt Bea of "The Andy Griffith Show" or Grandma Walton. Even on commercials older persons were depicted as childish and feeble, such as the "Where's the Beef?" lady, Clara Peller, in Wendy's commercials.

A great change is in the making—just look at today's older television stars. Joan Collins is the beautiful, powerful, and sexy Alexis Colby on "Dynasty." As reported in the Older Women's League's *OWL Observer*, "Today's older female characters wear negligees, kiss passionately, and have love affairs."[13] In fact, the pendulum has swung a bit too far, some argue, in portraying older characters a bit too glamorously. Other shows, such as "Golden Girls," depict more accurate characterizations.

Reaching the Older Customer Is Big Business

Marketing to reach the older consumer is another way in which attitudes toward older people are changing. More companies are realizing older consumers are a prime target because of their higher disposable income and their active lifestyles. In fact, the acronym to depict this new consumer, like the label for the consumer group identified as "yuppies," is now "OPALs"—Older Persons with Active Lifestyles.[14]

Major marketers are looking at new ways to identify and reach OPALs. The advertising agency J. Walter Thompson, for example, developed a method of consumer analysis that identifies consumer groups by stage of life, rather than by age or socioeconomic status.[15] A Chicago marketing research company, Goldring and Co., created several labels for the fifty-plus groups, which it identifies as the "Geromarket®." It reports six separate and distinctive

segments of older persons, each with characteristic attitudes, demographic profiles, and purchasing patterns. *The
Geromarket Study* defines these groups in the following
ways:

> **The Assureds.** Younger and more affluent than other
> groups . . . Mostly male, college-educated professionals
> . . . More likely to be employed than retired . . . In
> good health . . . Great deal of confidence in themselves
> and the future . . . Travel more than other segments . . .
> Use credit cards with considerable frequency . . . Several
> financial investments . . . Less likely to try new foods or
> beverages.
>
> **The Actives.** Best educated and most likely to be retired
> professionals . . . Live quietly on comfortable incomes
> but enjoy retirement in very active ways . . . Not espe-
> cially socially inclined or family oriented . . . Higher
> consumption rate of alcoholic beverages . . . Dine out
> frequently . . . Above average use of vitamins and min-
> erals . . . Drive foreign-made cars, usually compacts or
> subcompacts . . . More likely to ski than other groups,
> less likely to golf.
>
> **The Sociables.** Gregarious, adventurous, and young in
> spirit . . . Good joiners and volunteers . . . Entertain fre-
> quently . . . However, social life and relatively low in-
> come may cause problems . . . Buy now and pay
> later . . . Few investment holdings . . . Above average in
> purchases of alcoholic beverages . . . Dine out frequently
> at inexpensive restaurants offering senior citizen dis-
> counts . . . Drive large American-made cars . . . Prefer
> soap operas, game shows, sports, and late-night news.
>
> **The Contenteds.** Very well adjusted with many interests
> . . . Mainly older retired females . . . Well educated with
> average incomes and above-average net worth . . . Not
> impulsive, not looking for new challenges, not afraid of
> growing older . . . Family oriented, but not obsessively

so . . . Above-average ownership of investment instruments . . . Watches little television other than early news and "The Cosby Show" . . . newspaper and magazine readership . . . Frequent purchasers of shampoos and moisturizers.

The Concerneds. Least educated and lowest income group . . . Consumer with worries about money, health, the future, and growing older, but manage to maintain a positive attitude . . . Proud of their independence . . . Cope with environment by being thrifty . . . Look for promotions and bargains . . . Avid television watchers, window shoppers, and moviegoers . . . Patronize fast-food restaurants . . . Frequent purchasers of proprietary drugs and nutritional supplements . . . Plan to move to adults-only retirement communities more so than other groups.

The Insecures. Contradictory demographics . . . Fairly good income, but relatively low education . . . Negative outlook on life . . . Lack confidence in financial management and personal appearance . . . Few interests and unlikely to get involved with others . . . Participate in hunting, fishing, bowling, and golf . . . Above-average consumption of ice cream, frozen entrees, beer and liquor, but not wine . . . Frequent purchasers of aspirin, antacids, denture cleaners, liquid cold remedies . . . More likely than others to drive pick-ups or vans.[16]

No doubt about it, the older consumer market is big business. Because it is, corporations will find that by having older workers, older consumer issues can be addressed. Older customers generally shop where workers are attuned to their needs and concerns. Time and time again older shoppers are seen at the counter where an older worker is assisting them with their purchases. Older consumers buy products that meet their needs. Who understands the needs of older consumers better than other older individuals? By having older workers as an integral part of the work force, consumer needs will be more appropriately met.

Another way in which changing perceptions and attitudes is observed is the new wave of publications geared to the senior market. Magazine publishers are rushing to meet the "mature market" through a variety of publications meeting this market's needs:

- *Renaissance*, a monthly publication marketed by BHL Publishing.

- *Lifewise*, published by *American Health*.

- *50 Plus*, a publication purchased by *Reader's Digest*.

- *Lear's*, introduced by Francis Lear for the "woman who wasn't born yesterday."

- *Modern Maturity*, one of the three largest magazines in the United States, along with *Reader's Digest* and *TV Guide*. As the official publication of the American Association of Retired Persons, it has a readership of 16.7 million.

- *Longevity*, published by Omni Publications International, a consumer magazine.

- *Second Wind*, a "full life" publication.[17]

Obviously, publishers are recognizing the buying power of this powerful consumer group, and are providing a series of products to meet a growing market need. They recognize, as do marketing gurus, the diversity of this market segment.

However, even marketers are making mistakes about this population segment, reports Jeff Ostroff in his book, *Successful Marketing to the 50+ Consumer*. He tells of fallacies that deter those wanting to reach this fifty-plus market, and identifies "Eight Deadly Misconceptions":

- Mature adults are all the same.
- Mature adults think of themselves as old.
- Older adults aren't an important consumer segment.
- Mature adults won't try something new.
- Older persons have impaired mental facilities.
- Most older persons suffer from poor health.
- Older adults keep to themselves.
- Mature adults aren't physically active.[18]

Most of these same fallacies regarding older people as consumers can also be seen in attitudes toward older workers. Chapter 2 will further explore these myths about older workers, and will investigate the realities of the benefits in employing older workers.

In one study, however, corporate employers found that older workers were perceived "very positively" by those making employment decisions. Knowledge and experience were the factors that made older workers valuable to these employers, as well as attitudes of older workers toward work. In total, employers at 90 percent of the four hundred companies surveyed said they feel older workers are "cost effective" employees when all factors—such as salaries and insurance benefits—are considered. The only real concern raised in this survey was older workers' ability to adapt to "the technological and competitive requirements of current business."[19]

The older worker has come a long way in terms of perceptions in the business world. There no doubt will be increasing competition for these workers in the next years. Smart business leaders will be looking for ways to be competitive in the recruitment and retention of these workers.

Businesses' Response to the Aging Workplace

Just as marketers are changing their approach to the older consumer, employers must change their approach to the older worker. With issues such as labor shortages, increased labor costs, unskilled and inexperienced workers, and changing work ethics and values, it makes sense to take advantage of the wealth of experience and maturity the aging worker possesses. The older worker is more a part of the solution for employers than a problem.

How should businesses change to meet the changing and diverse needs of older workers and an aging work force? This question has been posed in several recent studies and reports.

One study, conducted by the American Society for Personnel Administration (now the Society for Human Resource Management) and Commerce Clearing House, revealed that while there are mixed views about older workers, there is a need for more policies and programs that will support the employment of older workers. "The availability of fewer entry-level workers, coupled with the trend among present workers to elect early retirement, could create serious staffing shortages in critical job categories," the report says.[20]

The report notes a tremendous difference in the need for policies and programs to support the employment of older workers, versus the existence of current guidelines for such employment.

Three government reports were released in January 1989 that outlined the government's increasing concern with labor shortages and older workers. One report said that a large potential labor shortage is imminent because the economy is projected to grow at 2 percent to 3 percent annually, while the work force is growing at just 1 percent. This report said most employers are aggressively pursuing members of the shrinking labor pool of younger workers while ignoring the special needs of older workers, which include flexible scheduling, job sharing, and health care. A second report, requested by then Labor Secretary Ann McLaughlin, studied trends among older workers, as well as ways to encourage later retirement. The third was requested by Congress and addressed problems faced by older workers.[21]

The Bureau of Labor Statistics study, titled *Labor Market Problems of Older Workers*, reached these specific conclusions:

- Many older workers want to find work, but find that they become discouraged because of age discrimination. Typically, average weeks of unemployment increases with age.

- Once older workers find new jobs, they usually suffer from greater earnings downgrades than do younger workers.

- The choice for many older workers is between full-time employment and retirement—no middle ground exists.

- Unemployment data on older workers are probably misleading, as they do not take into account those workers who become discouraged.[22]

The National Alliance of Business (NAB) has created a seminar series for business called "Invest in Experience." Its agenda for businesses to make the most of older workers includes these recommendations:

- Make recruitment and hiring practices age-neutral.

- Cater to older workers' lifestyles by offering flexible schedules.

• Offer benefit packages with options, such as cafeteria-type packages.

• Make lifelong learning a part of the organization.

• Adapt management attitudes to encourage the employment of older workers.

• Abolish age discrimination.[23]

Studies and reports all point to the fact that businesses need to rethink their approach to older workers, and must adopt policies and procedures that will accommodate recruiting and retaining these workers in the workplace. Recommendations for employers described in this book include the topics outlined next.

Analyze the market conditions, including labor shortages, that will affect the role of the older worker in the workplace. Business leaders must have a thorough understanding of the dynamics of the changing labor environment, and should develop resources to collect market data. Further, internal manpower planning is necessary to anticipate needs. Smart managers will analyze turnover data and retention rates on a regular basis to determine which programs and policies are the most effective in reaching corporate goals. This information will be critical in determining which programs are most productive in attracting and retaining specific employee populations, and which employee populations are most likely to meet corporate retention goals. By tracking and analyzing data, managers will be better able to make smart decisions about the employment of targeted labor populations, such as the older worker.

Understand the diversity of the older worker population— who they are and what they want. As can be seen in the examples from the Geromarket® study, the fifty-plus consumers are highly diverse, with differing values, needs, and concerns. This is also true of older workers. Specific segments with differing needs and motivations for work should be assessed by the employer. It is equally important to differentiate myths from realities in employing older workers, as many misperceptions still exist today. By understanding the pertinent demographic and sociographic information on this market segment, the employer can develop appropriate strategies to employ this group. Chapter 2 explores these issues, giving employers information on this unique market segment.

Use recruitment and selection strategies targeted to the older worker. Older job seekers, as they encounter age discrimination, become discouraged in their search. Because of this, they are more likely to respond to recruitment messages and activities that are targeted to an older audience— messages that tell that older candidate, "We want you!" Most corporate recruiters will admit that their company's recruitment literature rarely depicts an older worker, unless that worker is shown as part of senior management. Companies must communicate to the older worker that a mature worker is being sought for open positions. Chapter 3 examines ways employers can relay recruitment messages and design recruitment activities that attract these workers.

Fine-tune training and development programs to include plans for continued training and support for older workers. Many corporate training and development programs have been created for the younger worker, with very little regard given to the ongoing development needs of the older worker. As corporations try to keep pace in a technologically growing marketplace, specific strategies for updating the skills of older workers should be addressed. Chapter 4 reviews the training and retraining issues for these workers.

Develop compensation and pension plans to fairly reward and motivate the older worker. Older workers want and need different compensation programs. They value health insurance and life insurance more than their younger counterparts. They often need to work within Social Security guidelines so as not to jeopardize their benefits. They may have less need for money—or more need, depending upon their circumstances. Smart employers will develop pay plans and benefit programs that are flexible enough to meet the varying needs of this employee population. Chapter 5 offers suggestions for designing compensation programs that adequately reward and motivate senior employees.

Create an environment that is free of age discrimination, and that supports the home life/work life balance requested by older workers. Age discrimination can be as blatant as not interviewing candidates over a certain age, or can be as subtle as not providing job evaluations or retraining opportunities. It can also take the form of ageist language— language that is discriminatory. Whatever the form or shape age discrimination takes, employers must eliminate this archaic practice. Further, employers should look to nontraditional means to meet older workers' needs, including a myriad of alternative staffing strategies, such as flexible-scheduling, job-sharing, temporary assignments, part-time hours, and work-at-home arrangements, including telecommuting. Chapter 6 reviews guidelines for redesigning the workplace to effectively manage and retain a diverse work force.

Analyze retirement policies and preretirement programs to see that employee and corporate goals are being met. Many corporations have realized too late that early retirement policies cost the company valuable talent and experience. The all-or-nothing mentality of offering retirement as the

---

Businesses' Response to the Aging Workplace

- Analyze the market conditions, including labor shortages, that will affect the role of the older worker in the workplace.

  Chapter 1

- Understand the diversity of the older worker population—who they are and what they want.

  Chapter 2

- Use recruitment and selection strategies that are targeted to the older worker.

  Chapter 3

- Fine-tune training and development programs to include plans for continued training and support for older workers.

  Chapter 4

- Develop compensation and pension plans to fairly reward and motivate the older worker.

  Chapter 5

- Create an environment that is free of age discrimination and that supports the home life and work life balance requested by older workers.

  Chapter 6

- Analyze retirement policies and preretirement programs to see that employee and corporate goals are being met.

  Chapter 7

---

only option to full-time employment is counterproductive in an environment suffering from labor shortages. Progressive companies will offer options that permit older employees not only to plan for retirement, but also to balance work life and home life in a way that is meaningful to the employee and to the corporation. Chapter 7 outlines programs and policies that help older employees make educated decisions about work and retirement.

All these recommendations not only will make the workplace more conducive to the employment of older workers, but also will make the workplace better for all employees. For example, consider the corporation that developed a flexible staffing plan to entice older workers. This company found that flexible schedules not only helped attract and keep older workers, it also helped attract and keep dual-career couples, women with small children, and students. Another business found that by initiating a self-paced training program, older workers were able to learn more tasks in a more relaxed, comfortable environment. This same atmosphere made it easier for all workers to learn job-specific skills and tasks, and greatly improved morale in the training program.

In a labor-shortage environment, employers need to look for ways to retain key employees. Maintaining high morale, providing recognition and rewards, and responding to employee needs are just a few ways employers can do a better job of keeping employees. As a result, all employees will benefit and will be more likely to remain loyal to their employer, performing productively and efficiently. Meeting the needs of the aging work force not only becomes the solution to the problem, but also becomes the way to better manage human resources in general.

Notes

1. See Martha I. Finney, "Planning Today for the Future's Changing Shape," *Personnel Administrator*, January 1989, p. 44.
2. See Barbara Boyle Torrey, Keven G. Kinsella, Cynthia M. Taeuber, *An Aging World*, U.S. Department of Commerce, Bureau of the Census, July 1987, p. 4.

3. Ibid., p. 4.
4. See "U.S./Japan Summit Heralds Productive Aging," *The Alliance Reports*, Summer 1987, pp. 1, 7.
5. See John Case, "The Real Age Wave," *Inc.*, July 1989.
6. See "Researchers Predict Aged Population Will Outstrip Census Projections," *The Older Worker*, November 1988, pp. 7–8.
7. See *Older Workers: Prospects, Problems and Policies, 9th Annual Report*, National Commission for Employment Policy, Washington, D.C., Report No. 17, 1985, p. 9.
8. See "Questions and Answers: How Are Businesses Challenged by Age-Bias Suits?" *The Aging Workforce*, Vol. 1, No. 1, December 1987, p. 1.
9. See John S. DeMott, "Welcome, America, to the Baby Bust," *Time*, February 23, 1987, p. 28.
10. See Stephen J. Simurda, "Northeast Labor Shortage Forces Retailers to Bend the Rules," *Adweek's Marketing Week*, June 12, 1989, p. 24.
11. See *1988 ASPA Labor Shortage Survey*, American Society for Personnel Administration, Alexandria, Virg., p. 21.
12. See Martha I. Finney, "Learning is a job for life," *Personnel Administrator*, January 1989, p. 48.
13. See Sally Steenland, "More Older Women on Television, but Networks Avoid the Wrinkles," *OWL Observer*, January–February 1987.
14. See Bernie Ward, "The 'Gray Boom' in Marketing," *Sky*, June 1988, p. 48.
15. See Christine Donahue, "JWT Charts Consumers' Lifestyles," *Adweek's Marketing Week*, June 26, 1989, p. 3.
16. See Bernie Ward, "The 'Gray Boom' in Marketing," *Sky*, June 1988, pp. 54–55.
17. See Patrick Reilly, "Not-Mature Market," *Advertising Age*, June 13, 1988.
18. See Jeff Ostroff, "Eight Common Misconceptions" In *Successful Marketing to the 50+ Consumer*. (1989). Prentice-Hall Inc.: Englewood Cliffs, NJ. Used with permission.
19. See "Older workers rapidly becoming a new force in the labor market," *Resource*, August 1987, p. 2.
20. See "Study Finds Few Employer Programs for Aged," *The Older Worker*, August 1988, p. 4.
21. See "Studies urge hiring of elderly to ease labor crunch," *The Courier-Journal*, Friday, January 13, 1989.

22. See "McLaughlin Releases Six Task Force Reports in Farewell Press Conference," *Employment and Training Reporter*, January 18, 1989, p. 529.
23. See "An Agenda from NAB: How to Make the Most of Older Workers," *The Aging Workforce*, Vol. 1, No. 1, December 1987, p. 4.

2
The "New" Older Worker: A Profile

To me, old age is fifteen years older than I am.
                                    —Bernard M. Baruch

How old is "old"? Ask a group of preschool children, and they'll say their parents are old. Ask a group of teen employees, and they'll say anyone over thirty. Ask people in their thirties, and they'll say people in their sixties or seventies. And so it goes. We all think of old in terms of others, and usually those at least fifteen years older!

A recent Roper Poll asked, "What's 'old'?" Only 5 percent said forty to fifty-nine; 20 percent said sixty to sixty-nine; 31 percent said seventy to seventy-nine; 19 percent said eighty to eighty-nine; and 6 percent said ninety-plus.

In this country, people avoid being thought of as old because of the negative connotations associated with aging. Older people are thought of as over the hill or deadwood. No one wants to be thought of as older—consider the sixty-five-plus woman who walks up to a drugstore cashier and is asked if she qualifies for the senior citizen discount. She says "no" because she does not want to be labeled as an older person, even though it means she will not receive her discount. She is even a little angry that the cashier asked her this uncomfortable question!

When the term *older worker* is used, what does that mean? Is *older worker* appropriate? There is considerable debate as to what term is not only appropriate, but also preferred by older workers themselves. While the Age Discrimination in Employment Act (ADEA) is designed to protect individuals forty and older, and the federal Administration on Aging uses fifty-five and older for *older workers*, this book will refer to older workers as those employees aged fifty-plus.

Is *older worker* really the best term? Some would argue that *seniors* or *senior citizens* is preferred. However, while there has been wide acceptance of this term, *senior* generally means sixty-five and older. Just ask a group of fifty-five-year-olds if they are *senior citizens* and the answer will be made quite clear. The term *elderly* is even worse, as it tends to define those individuals seventy-five and older. And, while there may be some cause to speak of these "older-older" workers, most of the older workers are typically "younger-older" workers.

If the terms *seniors* and *elderly* are out, what other options are there? While the term *mature worker* has gained in popularity and is appropriate as it identifies those who are fifty-plus, it may imply that other workers are immature (even though some of these workers may fit that description!). Another positive term is *experienced workers*, but again, that implies that other workers are inexperienced.

It is important to recognize that labels used to describe these workers will tend to segment the market; in other words, describe a portion of the older worker population as opposed to the entire population. The significance of this point is apparent when businesses begin recruitment activities. For example, if *senior* is used in recruitment advertising, it will tend to attract people who are sixty-five-plus, and will not appeal to individuals younger than sixty-five. Therefore, the advertising will be limited in its appeal and effect. One food service corporation faced this dilemma when trying to attract older people to its work force. By saying in its recruitment messages, "We want seniors," it

Age and Identification Affiliation	
Mature Workers/Adults	50–65
Retired	55–70
Older Adults	55–70
Older Workers	60–75
Seniors/Senior Citizens	65–80+
Golden Agers	75–80+
Elderly	75–80+

failed to attract many candidates, and those few who did reply were over sixty-five. Refer to the box for terms used to identify older individuals, and the ages that are identified with each term.

Another point to consider is that people really do think of old age as fifteen years or so older than they are. Take the magazine *50 Plus.* Its average readership is sixty-two years of age—twelve years above the age the title implies—demonstrating that older adults tend to identify themselves with younger people. It is certain that employers need to exert caution in using any label that may differentiate or segment this older worker population.

Myths and Realities

The biggest barriers to the employment of older workers are myths about productivity, safety, and costs of employing these workers. Even in organizations in which business leaders are convinced that older workers make a positive, significant contribution, there are generally many individuals—typically supervisors, but often co-workers—who do not believe the older worker is a good worker. In fact, many companies that have initiated strong programs to em-

ploy mature workers also have developed sensitivity training programs to convince first-line supervisors and
co-workers that older workers as a group possess many
qualities that make them excellent workers. McDonalds'
"McMasters" program, Kentucky Fried Chicken's "Colonel's Tradition" and Hardee's "New Horizons" have all
incorporated manager training in an attempt to neutralize
some of these myths. Leaders of these programs have at-
tested to the success of introductory sessions for managers
in dispelling the stereotypes that are so prevalent.

What are the myths—and realities—of employing senior
workers? Outlined here are the primary concerns of employers.

Myth Number One: The perception by
business/customers of older workers is negative.

In a 1985 study by the marketing and social research firm
of Yankelovich, Skelly and White of human resource decision makers from four hundred companies, 72 percent said
experience, skill, and knowledge were strengths of older
workers. Older workers are consistently praised for their
dealings with customers, and often are placed in roles that
demand sensitivity to customer issues. One large department store found that sales increased when an older sales-
person waited on customers; one food service company
reported that customers often waited in line for their favor-
ite older cashier. One restaurant noted that its older customers were more likely to come in on days the older
hostess worked; they enjoyed the service as well as the
camaraderie of being with other older people.

Morris Massey, in his book *The People Puzzle: Understanding Yourself and Others* and in his training film
"What You are is Where You Were When . . . ," demonstrates that older workers—"traditionalists"—have a set of
work ethics and values consistent with excellent service. He

shows that many workers within this group value tact and diplomacy, especially more so than the younger workers he calls "challengers." He reports that traditionalists are willing to provide good customer service, as they value courtesy and good manners more than their younger counterparts.

*Myth Number Two: Older workers are less
productive than the average worker.*

Increasingly, research proves that chronological age is a poor predicter of physical or mental ability.[1] In one study, for example, it was found that levels of attainment for over-forty employees was as varied as with the young. This study concluded that if any correlation existed, it was that performance tended to *improve* with age.[2] The only documented declines in productivity reported are those from a 1965 study published by the Department of Labor that told of slight productivity declines for those workers older than forty-five who were performing heavy physical labor.[3]

In 1977 the U.S. Senate reported that workers sixty and older performed as well or better than their younger counterparts in quality and quantity. This study was conducted in more than three thousand retail, industrial, office, and managerial positions.[4]

A recent study conducted by the Institute for Social Research at the University of Michigan reported that older Americans participate in many unpaid productive activities that are comparable to middle-aged and younger Americans. It also demonstrated that men and women spend comparable time in productive work, even though the activities may vary from paid to unpaid.[5] This helps dispel the myth that older Americans are less productive than their younger counterparts.

Morris Massey also reports that the older "traditionalists" view work as a part of life, a duty, a responsibility—a strong work ethic. Younger workers, he says, look to work to be "fun." It would seem that older workers will really apply themselves to get the job done, valuing a hard day's work for a day's pay.

Myth Number Three: There's no need to hire and train older workers because they won't be on the job for long.

All in all, older workers are a better bet for retention. James Challenger, president of Challenger, Gray & Christmas, Inc., a Chicago-based outplacement consulting firm, reports that older workers tend to stay on the job for ten to fifteen years,[6] compared with AARP's report stating that younger workers ages twenty to thirty stay on the job 3.4 years.[7] Challenger notes that job tenure and company loyalty were extremely important following the Great Depression, as America became acutely aware of the value of a job. Because of these values, older workers tend to remain loyal to the company.

Others may argue that older workers remain on the job because they fear change, and because of that, a stable, secure workplace is of value. Whatever the underlying reason, employers have discovered that the older worker will more than likely remain long after the younger new hire is off to explore greener pastures.

Such is the case with Western Savings and Loan of Arizona and First Savings of San Diego. They continue to recruit older workers as tellers because of their high retention rates.[8]

Myth Number Four: Older workers don't want to climb the corporate ladder.

The truth is, older employees resent limits that are placed upon their ability to advance in their careers, just as their younger counterparts do, reports Dr. Max Bader, a Seattle-based medical consultant in preventive medicine.[9] He says people who reach sixty years of age have many more productive years, and that employers need to provide workers with the development tools to help them grow within their careers.

Many older workers find they can begin again in a second, third, or even fourth career, and want and expect the challenge of growth and development within that new career path. Take the example of Elaine, an older worker who, at the age of fifty-five, began a new career in food service. She began as an entry-level hourly worker, but was quickly promoted into her company's management training program as an assistant manager. After learning the ropes and proving her skills, abilities and judgment, she was promoted to manager. As one of the top managers within her area, she was again advanced, to the position of training manager—at the age of fifty-seven. Her managers tell of her unending enthusiasm and her ability to learn and grasp ideas quickly. Even though she had no experience in the industry (her background was in manufacturing) she was able to move up the corporate ladder to advance her pay and benefits, and remain challenged.

Myth Number Five: Older workers are inflexible and unwilling to change.

While many believe older people are more resistant to change, they are far from incapable of adjustment. Dr. Bader reports that older individuals may, in fact, be more cautious in light of their past experiences, which may be an advantage to employers. He says they may also be more willing to state objections. While some may perceive this trait as inflexibility, in certain cases this trait can be extremely valuable—for example, in a quality control manager. He also reports that flexibility is a personality trait that is developed in life's early stages, likely to remain constant throughout one's life, and not affected by the aging process.[10]

Myth Number Six: Most older individuals have adequate retirement income and do not need to work.

According to the American Association of Retired Persons, about 3.5 million elderly people were below the poverty level in 1985, with the poverty rate for persons older than sixty-five higher than for those younger than sixty-five (12.6 percent versus 14.1 percent). In total, over one-fifth, or 21 percent, of the older population were poor or near-poor in 1985.[11]

For some who retire with no pensions or small pensions, or for those who must rely on Social Security, the money is insufficient to support themselves and other family members. For others, while some support may be available, it is not adequate to provide the same quality of lifestyle that was enjoyed before retirement. Others may be forced into early retirement and may not yet be eligible for Social Security benefits. For many older Americans, there is a very real financial need to work.

Myth Number Seven: Older workers suffer from more illnesses and are absent from work more often than younger workers.

Statistics demonstrate that older workers have attendance records equal to or better than their younger counterparts. In fact, Dr. Bader reports that use of sick leave is more directly linked with life patterns of absences rather than with age.[12] Further, it appears that older workers who are less healthy tend to eliminate themselves from the workplace, leaving the healthier people to remain at work.

This appears to hold true at both Polaroid and Banker's Life: at Polaroid, 18 percent of older workers have perfect attendance, versus 10 percent for the total work force. Banker's Life has likewise found that its older workers have a 27 percent perfect attendance rate, as compared with 10 percent for its total work force.[13]

Tardiness records, as well as absenteeism records, are better for older workers than their younger counterparts. In fact, one common complaint from managers is that older workers often report in for work too early! What a nice problem to have!

Myth Number Eight: Older workers do not get along with co-workers.

According to the Cabinet for Human Resources, studies show that older workers are adept in interpersonal relationships, dependability, and job commitment.[14] Corporations with high percentages of younger workers are finding that older workers can be a tremendously stabilizing force. Many companies boast of older workers' acting as mentors and role models for younger workers.

In one such example, reported by a line manager of a national corporation, an older worker was hired and worked side-by-side with a much younger worker. The manager had high praise for the relationship, as the younger worker, unthreatened, showed the older worker the ropes, while the older worker listened to problems and concerns of the younger worker, offering advice and support.

Older people benefit from their lifelong experiences in dealing with and working with others. They learn how to hone their judgment and reasoning capabilities. As Grace Williams said, "We learn from experience. A man never wakes up his second baby just to see it smile."

*Myth Number Nine: It costs more to train an
older worker than it does other workers.*

For many jobs, it costs no more to train an older worker
versus other workers. While older workers respond best in
an environment that offers a self-paced training program,
almost *all* workers do best when this type of arrangement
can be offered. In those jobs in which training time is
longer for older workers, it has been proved that the investment is well worth it, with older workers remaining on the
job longer and performing as productively as younger
workers.

For certain jobs, older workers can learn certain roles
more quickly. Life experiences and work experiences teach
older workers to absorb new ideas and apply them more
readily—they can relate the concepts to past learning.

Older workers are more likely to complete their training
than their younger counterparts. And, because they are
more likely to stay with the company, the training investment pays off.

*Myth Number Ten: The costs of employee
benefits outweigh any gains from employing
senior workers.*

The Institute of Gerontology at the University of Michigan
reports that while there is a general impression that older
workers will cost employers more because of higher benefits use, especially for health care, this is not necessarily so.
One study conducted by The Travelers Companies showed
that older workers' and younger workers' costs varied, and
that no conclusion could be drawn about which group had
consistently higher costs.[15] A study by Yankelovich, Skelly,
and White, Inc. revealed that employers perceived health
benefits costs to be comparable for thirty-year-old males
and females with dependents and for sixty-five-year-old

male and female retirees. The study also revealed that health costs were perceived as less costly for fifty-five-year-olds than for the other groups.[16]

Even when costs are higher for older workers, many companies believe that the benefits they receive from the experience and skills of these workers more than makes up for any additional costs. Typically, when benefits costs are higher for older workers, the additional cost is a relatively low percentage of total benefits costs.

It has also been argued that overall employment costs are higher for older workers, especially when looking at higher rates of pay because of seniority. These costs are easily offset by lower turnover rates, resulting in lower recruiting and training costs.

Myth Number Eleven: Older workers are not motivated to work; they want to enjoy their retirement.

It is true that many older workers dream of retiring, and go on to retire and enjoy it immensely. However, there are many situations that motivate older persons to "unretire," keep on working, or even explore second or third career options. Some older people need to work for financial reasons; others want the challenge and excitement of work; others want the opportunity to work and share with other people; still others seek the gratification that comes from fulfilling a purpose.

Many older adults would like to enjoy a combination of work and retirement in a "semi-retirement" or "phased retirement" program. In this way older people can "try out" retirement, or can enjoy doing some of the fun things in life in a more balanced way. Many have found that being "retired" all day long is boring, yet working forty hours a week is too tiring and demanding. Part-time assignments are growing in popularity among older workers for this reason.

Myth Number Twelve: Older workers are more accident-prone and suffer more on-the-job accidents.

The reality is just the opposite. One report demonstrated that older workers account for only 9.7 percent of all workplace injuries, even though older workers make up 13.6 percent of the workforce. In another study, 1 million accidents were studied from the early 1980s, revealing that the accident rate for workers older than sixty-five was about half that of workers in their twenties.[17] A Bureau of Labor Statistics study revealed lower accident rates for older workers, which is particularly impressive given that in 1981 approximately 25 percent of older workers were employed in agriculture, mining, construction, and manufacturing occupations.[18] Older workers tend to be more careful in performing work assignments, and generally make fewer mistakes. Perhaps the old German proverb is true: "He who has burned his mouth blows his soup."

Myth Number Thirteen: Older workers will not want to work because it will jeopardize their Social Security benefits.

While many older workers receive Social Security benefits and want to manage their hours so as not to jeopardize these benefits, other older workers do not yet receive Social Security. Others may receive benefits, but find they can make more money working, or simply want to work for the enjoyment and satisfaction. In any case, employers need to talk with older workers to determine their needs, and should not make assumptions about their desires.

*Myth Number Fourteen: Older workers are not
as intellectually adept.*

Many studies of intellectual functioning indicate that intelligence remains intact for most people until the age of seventy, and for many, beyond that point. And, as those who are working tend to be healthier than those who aren't, they are more likely to remain mentally alert and active. In addition, many abilities, such as judgment and decision making, combined with general knowledge, tend to increase with age.[19] Even those older workers who do suffer from reduced short-term and long-term memory compensate for this loss by not guessing as much, thus eliminating many mistakes.[20]

*Myth Number Fifteen: Older people who can't
find jobs don't have the experience and
qualifications.*

Often, senior job seekers lack confidence in their skills and abilities. They also fear (and many times, rightly so) age discrimination. However, what older workers lack in confidence they certainly make up for in work and life experience. Even those who have not worked outside the home possess a wealth of life experiences in dealing with projects, people, and priorities.

Clearly, after comparing the myths and realities of employing older workers we see that older workers are not just solutions to the problems facing employers today, but are *excellent* solutions! Employing older workers is smart business in today's difficult labor environment.

Demographics

To better design policies, procedures, and programs to recruit, train, manage, and retain the older worker, it is help-

Older Workers: Myths and Realities

The myth is that older workers . . .

- are viewed negatively by customers

- are slow, unproductive workers

- won't be with the company long

- don't want to advance

- are inflexible and resistant to change

- don't need to work

- are absent from work because of illness

- are difficult to work with

- are expensive to train

- incur higher insurance costs

- are not interested in work

- are more accident-prone

- won't work because of Social Security benefits

- are not as adept intellectually

- lack experience

The reality is that older workers . . .

- are viewed positively by customers

- are as productive as their younger counterparts

- remain on the job longer than younger workers

- want to learn and grow

- are willing to change and adapt

- may need the money

- have fewer incidences of absence and tardiness

- are adept in interpersonal relationships

- repay the training investment quickly

- may cost no more to insure

- are motivated to work

- have fewer on-the-job accidents

- may need additional income, or want to work

- are intellectually adept

- have a wealth of life experiences

ful to understand more about who older people are, how they feel about work and retirement, and what they perceive to be the incentives and barriers to work.

The Older Population

People sixty-five and older numbered 28.5 million in 1985, representing 12 percent of the U.S. population. Of that figure, 2.9 million participate in the work force.[21] Of those, 1.7 million are men and 1.2 million are women. There are 11.9 million people fifty-five to sixty-four participating in the work force, with 7 million men and 4.9 women.[22] Refer to figure 2–1.

From this information we see there is a dramatic drop in participation rates for those older than sixty-five. Businesses can benefit by investigating strategies to attract more

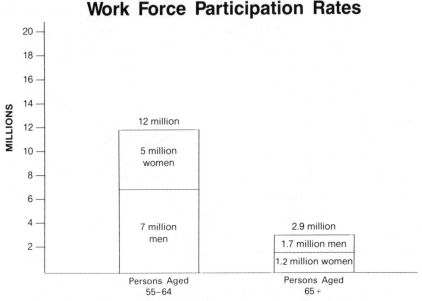

Source: Adapted from "A Profile of Older Americans," American Association of Retired Persons, Washington, DC, 1986, p. 1; and from "Workers 45+: Today and Tomorrow," American Association of Retired Persons, Washington, DC, 1986, p. 4.

Figure 2–1. *Work Force Participation Rates*

of these people back into the work force. Also, it is apparent that the participation rate for women in the work force is lower than men in the fifty-five-to-sixty-four age bracket. There may also be some specific strategies to draw these women into the workforce, which will be discussed in chapter 3 on recruitment and in chapter 6 on management and retention.

Since 1975, participation rates for men and women in age brackets fifty-five-to-sixty-four and sixty-five-plus have continued to decline, except for women in the fifty-five-to-sixty-four age bracket.[23] This may imply that women in this "younger-older" age bracket could be an excellent target market for employers to identify for recruitment.

Older People and Poverty

Many of the nation's elderly live in poverty. About 3.5 million elderly were below the poverty level in 1985, with the poverty rate at 12.6 percent, less than the rate for people younger than sixty-five (14.1 percent). In total, over one-fifth, or 21 percent, of the older population were poor or near-poor in 1985.[24]

Older women were more likely to be poor than older men, and had a considerably higher poverty rate than men (16 percent versus 8 percent) in 1985.[25]

Businesses that want to attract more older workers will find that women, because of the high incidence of poverty, will be a top target for employment opportunities because of their need. Many older people have a great financial need for work—a strong motivation to use to bring these individuals back into the workforce.

Women as Older Workers

The work patterns of women early in life affect their ability to earn salary and benefits later in life. Because women spend so much of their lives in low-paying jobs, often without benefits, they become more economically vulnerable than men. While many women—over half—aged forty-five to sixty-five work for pay, and an amazing 70 percent work full time, only about 40 percent are vested in pension plans.[26]

Older women also are more likely to rely on Social Security than men, receive lower Social Security benefits, and be renters. They are less likely to be homeowners.

Women are more likely to make long-term commitments to their jobs and are less likely to job-hop. For example, for every woman who retired in 1980 and 1981, one-third reported working for one employer for at least twenty years. According to the AARP, at age fifty, women are likely to work for fifteen years of service for one employer.

Older women, fifty-five-plus, now make up 40 percent of the older workers, reports Diane Herz of the Bureau of Labor Statistics.[27] These women work in the three traditional female job categories: sales, administrative support (which includes clerical), and services.

In a recent AARP roundtable discussion with thirteen agencies and businesses that were interested in the concerns of older women workers, key issues were discovered that need to be addressed by employers. Women aged fifty-plus want challenging work, appropriate skills training, an environment free of discrimination, adequate retirement benefits, and assistance with pre-retirement planning.

There are obvious opportunities and challenges in employing older women. They offer commitment, loyalty, and a wealth of skills and experience. However, because they often live longer and healthier, and are poorer, employers must look at strategies to eliminate discrimination and offer a satisfying work experience.

Occupations

More older workers aged sixty-five-plus are employed in occupations that fall within the category of technical, sales, and administrative positions. The second-highest occupation represented by those aged sixty-five-plus is in managerial and professional, followed by service. Workers fifty-five to sixty-four are similarly employed most in technical, sales, and administrative occupations and managerial and professional occupations. However, they are represented third in the occupational category of operators, fabricators, and laborers. The occupations with the highest percentage of workers forty-five-plus are in farming, forestry, and fishing, with 35 percent represented.[28]

Implications for businesses with occupations in which older people are strongly represented are that these are positions that traditionally have appealed to and attracted older persons, giving these businesses the best opportunity to continue to attract and retain older workers. For occupations with low representation of older workers, businesses will need to investigate methods to attract older persons through stronger recruitment programs, redesign of key positions, elimination of discriminatory practices, and more creative staffing alternatives.

Perceptions of Work

In 1983, the AARP conducted a survey of older individuals aged fifty-five-plus that asked how they would identify their current employment status. Thirty-seven percent of those responding said they were working either full time or part time. A whopping 48 percent said they were retired, and only 2 percent said they were unemployed. Twelve percent said they were homemakers; 2 percent said they were disabled. A recap of this information can be seen in the box.

Self-Perception of Work Status by Persons Aged 55+

Retired 48%
Work full-time 26%
Homemaker 12%
Work part-time 11%
Unemployed 2%
Disabled 2%

Source: American Association of Retired Persons

Employers may first be concerned at the low number of people who considered themselves to be unemployed, as this indicates that a majority of older persons are not actively seeking employment. However, there is reason to believe that the numbers of those saying that they are retired may be inflated because of the social acceptance of the term. In the same way that many people do not say, "I'm unemployed," but say instead, "I'm between opportunities," many older persons say they are "retired." There is also reason to believe that many persons who are retired may consider returning to the workforce. In fact, studies have shown that one out of three retirees would return to work if offered the right job opportunity, reports Greg Newton, president of Newton & Associates, a consulting firm that works with nonprofit and public organizations in employment and marketing strategies. Newton says that just because older people report they are retired does not necessarily mean that their income is sufficient, or that they are satisfied with retirement.

For those who indicated that they were homemakers, this again may be more an indication of traditional values, Newton says. This response may not truly indicate a lack of interest in paid-work opportunities, but rather an acceptable term for women, as "retired" is for men.

Employers should recognize from these data that many older people who are not currently working are not actively seeking employment. It is rare for an older person to come knocking on the employment door. Rather, businesses interested in attracting these workers need to develop recruitment strategies that reach out to older individuals during the course of their daily activities. Chapter 3 will discuss in detail such strategies.

Employers should also be aware that many older persons will need to be "sold" on the opportunities of working. Because of the social acceptance of retirement, many will need to be shown how work can improve the quality of their life.

In this same AARP survey, older employees who were working either full time or part time were asked, "If you could afford it, would you rather retire, or are you glad to be still working?" Seventy-four percent said they prefer work over retirement; 21 percent said they would like to retire. Slightly more women than men preferred to work (77 percent versus 71 percent). People sixty-five to sixty-nine were very interested in continuing to work (81 percent), and people seventy-five-plus had the strongest interest in working (93 percent!).

It would appear that as people continue to work past age fifty-five, they do so out of a conscious choice. This study also indicates that many older people feel they must continue to work for financial reasons.

In fact, this AARP survey also asked retirees if they were glad they retired, or if they would rather be working. Those with the lowest income levels indicated a higher interest in working, and those with highest income levels indicated the lowest interest in working.

In a 1981 Louis Harris poll, adults eighteen to eighty-plus were asked their opinions about work and retirement.

Ninety percent of the respondents agreed that "Nobody should be forced to retire if he/she wants to work and can still do a good job." And while 69 percent said they would prefer to retire at or after sixty-five, 79 percent of those fifty-five to sixty-four, and 73 percent of those sixty-five-plus, would prefer working part time instead of retiring completely.[29]

Businesses can benefit from this information by understanding that many older people could be retained in the work force through part time work and other flexible scheduling arrangements.

In fact, the AARP's Worker Equity Department has found that the best incentives that might keep a person at work past retirement age include flexible work schedules, part-time work arrangements, and temporary employment. (See table 2–1.)

The Diversity of Older People

Older people are the most heterogeneous population segment when lifestyles, values, motivations for work, and

Table 2–1
Incentives that might keep a person at work past retirement age

(percent of survey sample)

	Women	Men
Flexible schedules	50	39
Part-time employment	44	38
Temporary employment	41	31
Phased retirement	38	34

Source: Adapted from AARP Worker Equity Department survey appearing in "How to entice older people to give up early retirement and keep on working," *The Older Worker*, June 1988, pg. 2.

other variables are compared. Some have likened the aging process to a fan: As aging occurs, we open up, becoming more unique and different. So, while it is possible to characterize older people as having this trait or that quality, it is important to recognize the differences.

Studies that demonstrate the diversity of this age group have grown in number as the older population becomes increasingly important to marketers and others. For example, William E. Becker, president of William E. Becker Organization, a New Jersey developer of retirement communities, reported at a recent conference of the American Demographics that there are distinct differences between the needs of people fifty-five to sixty-four, and people seventy-five and older. The Geromarket® study discussed in chapter 1 also highlights the diversity of older persons.

Another study, sponsored by the National Association for Senior Living Industries (NASLI), demonstrates the diversity of older persons. Lifestyles and Values of Older Adults analyzed psychology, socioeconomics, and health factors, and developed six older-adult market segments. While these segments were intended to allow retirement housing decisions to be studied, the results can help business leaders understand the differences in the types of older workers and their corresponding motivations for work.

The six segments are: (1) Explorers, (2) Adapters, (3) Pragmatists, (4) Attainers, (5) Martyrs, and (6) Preservers.[30] The key psychographic components of each distinctive group are outlined next.

Explorers. These people are more self-reliant, independent, and introverted. They are individualists, with a strong sense of autonomy and tendencies toward self-denial. They are more likely to believe that children do not have an obligation to care for their parents. Explorers have an average household income, are in moderately better health, are slightly younger, and typically are high school graduates.

Adapters. These people are fairly well educated, with an average of two years of college. They are extroverted and more open to change, and often are considered the sociables in a group. This segment is second only to Attainers in terms of health, wealth, and self-indulgence. Adapters, however, are very dependent upon others.

Pragmatists. Pragmatists represent a large portion of the fifty-five-plus population, with the second-highest median age of all the segments. They possess an average median income, and typically have completed grade eleven. They are more likely than most to live alone, and are conservative and conformist in values. They are average in their receptivity to change.

Attainers. These people make up the healthiest, wealthiest, most independent, and most self-indulgent segment. They are often the youngest and, with Adapters, have the best educations. They are achievement-driven and, like Explorers, feel that children do not have an obligation to support parents.

Martyrs. Martyrs make up the largest group, with about 26 percent of the fifty-five-plus population falling into this segment. They are among the youngest (with Attainers), and have the second-lowest income level and second-lowest educational level. This segment is more introverted, most self-denying, and most resistant to change. It tends to be the most helpless of all the groups.

Preservers. This segment is the oldest of the groups, and is typically the least healthy—more respondents who were

disabled fell into this category. They have the lowest household income, and the lowest educational level. They are
highly resistant to change. They are need-driven, and their
main goal is to preserve what little they possess.[31]

Several key points become obvious to the employer in
reviewing these segments:

- Each group is different in its values, needs for employment, and lifestyles.

- Because of the diversity of these segments, no single
  strategy for recruitment, management, or retention will
  be effective in employing older persons.

- A variety of policies and programs will need to be developed by employers interested in attracting older
  people.

- There may be some opportunity to target subsegments
  of the older population for more effectiveness in employment strategies.

For example, Preservers, because of their low income levels,
may be more motivated to work because of financial need,
yet may be hard to recruit because of their resistance to
change, or because of their poor health. Attainers may be
excellent for positions that require higher educational levels; however, they may be less likely to desire work because
of their higher income levels.

Employers will need to rethink not only how they perceive older persons, but also how they develop policies and
programs that will respond to each of these population subsets. Recruitment messages and activities that appeal to Explorers, for example, may be quite different from those that
attract Adapters. Employment policies that will be viewed
favorably by Preservers may be only a neutral to Attainers.
Employers who want to be most effective in employing

Older Worker Profile: Facts and Opportunities

Fact	Opportunity
• There is a dramatic drop in labor force participation rates for older workers.	• Investigate strategies to retain older persons in the workforce.
• Older women are more likely to remain in the labor force.	• Develop policies and procedures to entice older women to remain in the workforce.
• Many older persons live in poverty—more women than men.	• Attract older persons to meet their financial needs, especially women.
• Women are loyal workers; they have many reasons to continue to work.	• Offer challenging work, skills training, benefits, pre-retirement planning.
• Older workers are more often employed in technical, sales, and administrative positions.	• Develop strategies to retain workers in these occupations, and entice workers to explore new careers in other occupations.
• Many older persons consider themselves to be "retired" or "homemakers"; few think of themselves as "unemployed."	• Use outreach strategies to attract older persons in the course of their daily activities.
• Workers want more flexibility in work.	• Create more scheduling alternatives, such as part-time, temporary, and flex-schedules.
• Older persons are a diverse population.	• Initiate a variety of policies, programs, and activities to attract and retain older workers.

older workers must think more like marketing professionals in targeting the market segments and applying programs that meet the needs of these segments.

Facts and figures on older persons and their thoughts and feelings about work, retirement, lifestyle, motivation, and need for work have been explored in this chapter, revealing many opportunities for businesses to respond. These opportunities are outlined in the box. Each of the following chapters will use this information in detailing specific strategies to recruit, select, orient, train, compensate, manage, and retain older workers for a workplace that needs these workers.

Notes

1. See David Nye, *Alternative Staffing Strategies*, The Bureau of National Affairs, Inc., Washington, D.C., 1988, p. 120.
2. See Peter Naylor, "In praise of older workers," *Personnel Management*, November, 1987, p. 47.
3. See David Nye, pp. 120–121.
4. See Pauline K. Robinson, "Research Update: The Older Worker," *Generations: Quarterly Journal of the American Society on Aging*, 1982.
5. See "Older Workers Study Completed," *Aging Network News*, October 1989, p. 6.
6. See James E. Challenger, "Older Workers Teach Stability," *Recruitment Today*, May/June 1989, p. 22.
7. See David Nye, p. 117.
8. Ibid., p. 117.
9. See Max Bader, "Attitudes Harden Before Arteries When Hiring the Elderly," *Wall Street Journal*, June 6, 1988.
10. Ibid.
11. See "A Profile of Older Americans," American Association of Retired Persons, Washington, D.C., 1986, p. 10.
12. See Max Bader.
13. See David Nye, p. 116.
14. See "Older Workers: Myths & Reality," Cabinet for Human Resources, Department for Employment Services.

15. Ibid.
16. See David Nye, p. 120.
17. See Dorothy Dee, "Older Workers: The industry workforce of the future?" *Restaurants USA*, Sept. 1987, pp. 10–11.
18. See David Nye, p. 117.
19. Ibid., p. 117.
20. See Peter Naylor.
21. See "A Profile of Older Americans," American Association of Retired Persons, Washington, D.C., 1986, p. 1.
22. See "Workers 45 + : Today and Tomorrow," American Association of Retired Persons, Washington, D.C., 1986, p. 4.
23. Ibid., p. 5.
24. See "A Profile of Older Americans," American Association of Retired Persons, Washington, D.C., 1986, p. 10.
25. Ibid., p. 11.
26. See "What Older Women Workers Want and Need," The *Older Worker*, May 1988.
27. See "As Men Continue to Retire Early, Many Firms Must Look to Older Women Workers," *The Older Worker*, October 1988.
28. See "Workers 45 + : Today and Tomorrow," American Association of Retired Persons, Washington, D.C., 1986, p. 7.
29. Ibid., p. 19.
30. See James Gollub and Harold Javitz, "Six Ways to Age," *American Demographics*, June 1989, p. 30.
31. Ibid., pp. 30–56.

3
Hiring Experience: Attracting and Selecting Older Workers

If you always do what you always did, you'll always get what you always got.

—Unknown

F inding and attracting older workers is different in today's labor environment; in fact, finding and attracting any worker in a labor-shortage market can be a much more involved process than the tried-and-true methods used in the past. No longer are candidates responding to newspaper help-wanted advertisements or applying in person for an open position. Employers must use more creative and aggressive strategies for attracting all workers in this new labor environment, particularly for older workers.

New Staffing Principles

In a number of ways recruiting must be different today than in the past. These new principles for labor-shortage environments are discussed next.

Segment the targeted recruiting market and direct recruiting messages to that audience. Just as successful marketers understand that the most effective marketing messages are those targeted to a specific population, successful recruiters are learning these same lessons. Recruiting messages are most effective when the target population is clearly identified, and when specific messages are designed for that market segment.

Use messages that sell. What does the job candidate want and need? Recruitment messages should include terminology that clearly shows job candidates that their needs will be met by answering the advertisement. This means advertisements should include information on the features, advantages, and benefits of working for the employer—and not just information on the job qualifications. Job benefits should detail more than health insurance or vacation pay; they should include information on job rewards, satisfiers, growth potential, training opportunities, and other tangible and intangible benefits.

Recruitment messages also should sell the way product messages sell—by using graphics, pictures, and creative jingles and copy. While recruitment messages should avoid being too gimmicky, they can be fun, and definitely should entice the audience.

Make it easy for job candidates to explore the job opportunity. In the past, candidates were asked to apply for jobs within very specific guidelines. For example, it was not unusual to request job candidates to apply, in person, between 2:00 and 3:00 P.M., Thursdays only, with a résumé. The candidate who worked elsewhere would have to sneak away from work or call in sick to apply for another job. This process actually made it easier for unemployed candidates to apply than employed candidates. The philosophy was, "If they want the job bad enough, they'll do whatever it takes to get here."

Today, employers are offering easy access to the staffing

door. Some make available a twenty-four-hour employment "hot line" so that candidates can easily call to obtain information on available positions. Others are opening their doors on evenings and weekends. Some employers are even including a "mini-application" with the newspaper advertisement, allowing candidates without a résumé to respond immediately. By providing easy access for application and information, the employer is better able to attract candidates who otherwise might not have applied.

Treat job candidates like customers—they are shopping for a job. How well are candidates treated in the employment process? Traditionally, not well. They wait for hours for a scheduled interview, they never receive a follow-up call, or they are told, "Don't call us, we'll call you." What customer would tolerate that kind of treatment when there are so many other alternatives?

Job candidates should receive excellent treatment, as this is the first way in which the employer has the opportunity to make a positive impression. Appointments should be prompt; followup information should be communicated to candidates quickly; thank-you letters should acknowledge every résumé and application. Some employers, including Disney World in Lake Buena Vista, Florida, use "mystery shoppers" to pose as job applicants to ensure that all job candidates get the kind of first-rate treatment that all guests at Disney receive.

Create the right image with candidates—don't send a "desperation" message. When help-wanted advertisements appear in the newspaper week after week after week, it sends a message to job candidates that says, "Our company is desperate for help." And, while the organization may feel desperate, it does not want to send this message. Like the home buyer who sees the home listing in the multiple listing book week after week, job candidates begin to wonder, "What's wrong with it?" Avoid sending too many recruitment messages to the same audience.

Collaborate to achieve corporate goals. In today's labor market it can be quite difficult to achieve corporate goals independently. Many smart employers are working with government agencies and organizations to provide assistance in recruiting and selecting qualified applicants.

Be competitive. Know and understand the competitive marketplace when it comes to employment issues. In a highly competitive labor market it is important to understand who the competition is, and what it is offering to candidates in terms of compensation, benefits, and other tangible and intangible rewards. It is also imperative to know what recruitment activities and messages are being used elsewhere if you want to plan and implement effective recruitment programs.

Be imaginative and creative in planning recruitment messages and activities. Many times, tried-and-true methods are not effective today. When traditional methods no longer work, it's time to look to product and service marketing for fresh ideas. Telemarketing, direct mail, radio, and television are all strategies that have been used effectively in the marketing arena, and are being discovered by recruitment managers. By using a nontraditional approach, employers are able to remain competitive by attracting top candidates.

Use a variety of methods to achieve goals. The expression "Don't put all your eggs in one basket" is especially appropriate in approaching recruitment activities. It is unlikely that any one strategy will be effective in solving all of the recruitment issues. By using a variety of methods, goals can be better achieved.

Be persistent! Employment managers and recruiters need to be persistent in the marketplace to get top candidates. It also becomes more important to plan ahead for future openings, rather than to merely react to vacancies as they occur. By applying pro-active manpower planning principles and by using ongoing recruitment strategies, employers will be able to attract the quality and quantity of candidates needed.

Recruiting Older Workers

How do these recruiting principles for today's labor environment affect the way employers attract older workers? If employers are going to be effective in outreach activities to older adults, new recruiting principles must be applied. Let's explore in depth each of these principles to understand how employers can most readily recruit older workers.

Segment the older adult market. Older adults want to know that they are being targeted in recruitment messages. Often, because of age discrimination, many older adults feel they are not wanted in the workplace. Therefore, messages should be designed that speak directly to them.

One way in which employers effectively target the message to older adults is through testimonial advertisements. Depiction of an older adult, either by artwork or a picture, tells older worker candidates that this ad is meant for them. Avoid funny cartoons, however, since older adults may be turned off by these messages. By including a message targeted to older candidates, the advertisement gains

Figure 3–1. *Focus on Esteem Need.*

How to ease back into the labor pool

With our friendly, supportive team and thorough training program, you'll be surprised how quickly your skills and confidence will grow. You can work full- or part-time, with flexible hours. Excellent pay and benefits: pension and savings plans, health and life insurance, free uniforms, great discounts on meals, and outstanding advancement opportunities. Apply now at:

Hardee's®
We're out to win you over.℠

Hardee's is an Equal Opportunity Employer

Figure 3–2. *Focus on Security Need.*

Social Security leave you socially insecure?

Give your income and your life a boost with a part-time job at Hardee's. You can limit your hours so your Social Security benefits aren't cut, and still be part of our fun, friendly team. Excellent pay and benefits include health and life insurance, company-matched savings plan, free uniforms, and great discounts on meals. Apply now at:

Hardee's®
We're out to win you over.℠

Hardee's is an Equal Opportunity Employer

Figure 3–3. *Focus on Financial Need.*

Relish
your retirement
years

If you like people and want to stay active, come work part-time at Hardee's. You can limit your hours so your Social Security benefits aren't cut. Excellent pay and benefits include health and life insurance, free uniforms, and great discounts on meals. Apply now at:

Hardee's®
We're out to win you over.℠

Hardee's is an Equal Opportunity Employer

Figure 3–4. *Focus on Social Need.*

credibility and power. For example, an ad showing an older man or woman, saying in the ad copy, "I'm retired . . . but now I'm learning and meeting new friends in my new job at XYZ Company," will appeal to many older persons who may also have retired and be attracted to a work environment with other older persons.

Avoid, however, direct identification by age in ads. For many older persons, a specific age focus can be offensive. Instead, use messages that focus on their needs and concerns.[1]

Depicting older adults in recruitment advertising can be a strong tool. Many have said that recruitment literature that includes pictures of employees, without pictures of older adults, is an indication that the organization is not really interested in older adults as employees.

As discussed in chapter 2, studies have indicated that the senior market is a highly diverse market, with many submarkets. Employers have also benefited by identifying the subsegment of older adults in which it has the most interest, and then designing recruitment messages for that specific segment. For example, if employers believed that the subgroup of Explorers, described in the psychographic analysis, was the best group for recruitment because the job required socially oriented people, a recruitment message that appealed to that social orientation might be effective. Examples of such messages include: "Join With Others," "Meet New People," or "Join Our Team." Other employers may be interested in attracting Attainers, and could use messages such as, "Achieve Even More in Your Next Career," or "Be All That You Can Be—In A New Career." Recruitment activities can also be targeted. For example, for those seniors who are looking for a way to work with others and meet new people, a recruitment open house or "unretirement" party might be very appealing, as opposed to a one-on-one interview appointment.

Recruitment Messages

Motivation for Work	Recruitment Message
• Financial need	• "Work and still keep your Social Security benefits."
	• "You raised your family, now raise some cash."
	• "Make top pay and benefits."
• Security need	• "Work with a leader in the industry."
	• "We offer stability."
	• "We have never laid off an employee."
• Social need	• "Meet and make new friends."
	• "Join our friendly team."
	• "Come to work with people just like you."
• Esteem need	• "We value your experience and judgment."
	• "We want people like you."
	• "Come and work where you will be appreciated."

Recruitment Activities

Motivation for Work	Recruitment Activities
• Financial need	• Information seminars and open houses including financial planning
	• Print recruitment ads stressing pay and benefits
• Security need	• Direct mail piece that conveys the corporation's longevity
	• Recruitment literature with information on the parent company
• Social need	• "Bring a friend" campaign for on-site interviews or open house
	• "Unretirement" party with a direct mail piece as the invitation
	• Employee referral program/older worker task force
• Esteem need	• One-on-one confidential needs assessment after an open house
	• Telemarketing campaign that stresses the value of experienced workers

---

Sell recruitment messages to the senior market. To sell to the senior market, employers must understand the wants and needs of this population. First of all, many older persons perceive a variety of barriers to employment, among them being:

- "I'm not wanted because of my age."
- "I can't learn."
- "I can't compete."
- "I don't have transportation."
- "I can't physically handle the job."[2]

Therefore, employers should directly address these concerns in recruitment messages.

Employers have learned that older adults want the following from a work environment:

- An environment free of age discrimination.
- A flexible work schedule that permits part-time or temporary work, and other flex-schedules.
- A supportive work environment.
- An employer who values their experience and maturity.
- Fair compensation for their work.
- Benefits that meet their needs.

The organization is more likely to attract these workers if it includes this information in recruitment literature.

While many older worker candidates are attracted by different messages based upon their motivation for work, lifestyle, and other variables, the following messages are very effective in attracting older adults, reports Greg Newton, President of Newton & Associates.

- Your skills, experience, and maturity are valued.
- Join other mature individuals—just like you.
- Flexible hours—the hours you want to work.

- Job accommodation to meet your needs.

- You can work and still keep your Social Security—we help you manage your work hours.

- Stay active—and keep young.

- An opportunity to make new friends . . . in a friendly place.

- A growth opportunity . . . for your second or third career.

- Fringe benefits—especially health and life insurance.

- You already have the skills and experience to do the job.

- No training required.

- On-the-job training provided.

- Keep on giving—help others.

- Now that you have raised your family . . . raise some cash.

- Did you retire too soon?

While each of these messages can be effective, one of the best is "Did you retire too soon?" because it can attract many persons with a wide variety of backgrounds. For example, some older people may have retired too soon, and now they cannot afford to do the things they want to do. Some have retired and now are bored, or are lonesome for the companionship of others.

One way that employers can effectively sell the recruitment message to older candidates is to design a recruitment action plan that details the specific market segment along with the messages and activities that will accomplish this task. A sample of a planning sheet is provided in the box.

Targeting the Market: Recruitment Strategy Planning Sheet

Describe the candidate who will be most successful in the position.

Age: _____

Sex: _____

Location: _____

Lifestyle: _____

Values: _____

Needs: _____

What does this candidate need and value? What recruitment messages will appeal to this candidate?

_____

_____

_____

_____

What is this candidate doing? Where? What recruitment activities will be most effective?

_____

_____

_____

Provide easy access for older candidates to explore the employment opportunities. Many job candidates are uneasy about interviews, especially older candidates. Often, older persons have been out of the job market, and are uneasy about reentry procedures. Some older people have held one job for a long time, and have not gone through the job search process in ten, twenty, or even thirty years. The prospect of applying for a job can be unnerving.

Therefore, employers must work doubly hard to ensure that job opportunities are easily accessible to older candidates. Some suggestions for ways in which employers can ease job search pains include the following:

- Add an employment "hot line" that offers detailed job information. This can be accomplished as easily as installing a telephone answering machine with a recorded message that is changed weekly.

- Offer a clip-out mini-application form within the newspaper help-wanted advertisement. This assists the candidate who does not have a prepared résumé.

- Offer a brochure with additional job information that can be requested by interested candidates.

- Include a tear-off mini-application form with posters about employment information.

- Offer "team" interviewing, allowing the older candidate to bring a friend who might also be interested in job opportunities.

- Plan open houses and career fairs especially designed for older candidates.

All these strategies give candidates an opportunity to explore job options in a nonthreatening atmosphere. Each strategy can be tailored for older candidates exclusively, for more effective targeting of this market segment.

Treat older candidates like customers. Most older worker candidates are like the window shopper who goes to the mall just to look, and may buy something if it is appealing. Older candidates are not actively looking for a job, as was discussed in chapter 2; only 2 percent of older people consider themselves unemployed and are actively seeking employment. A larger percentage might consider the right opportunity if it presented itself. Because many older candidates are "just shopping," employers must do their best to treat these potential employees as well as they treat their valued customers.

The first place an employer has an opportunity to treat the older candidate well and to create a positive first impression is with the person who answers the phone for the employer. Does the receptionist answer all calls promptly and courteously? Are employment calls directed quickly and courteously to the appropriate person? Is the receptionist informed about employment opportunities? Is the older caller, as well as all callers, treated as if an employment inquiry is very important to the company? Many older people may become discouraged early in the employment process if this first encounter is not a positive one.

The employment office should also take great pains to be responsive to older job candidates. Letters should be sent to all walk-in applicants, and to those who send in a résumé, indicating that the résumé or application has been received. Interview appointments should be conducted on time, and followup schedules need to be adhered to by those making the hire decision.

To ensure that all candidates, especially older workers, are receiving the best treatment possible, the following guidelines should be met:

• Periodically call in anonymously and talk with those who answer the phone. How are applicants treated?

- Hire a mystery shopper to test the employment process. Is the candidate treated well throughout the system?

- Develop a system to respond to all résumés and applications. If a large number is received, consider using a preprinted card thanking all applicants for their interest and advising them of the employment process. Using a word processing system or data base system for applicant information can be another way to give prompt service to candidates. This is being used successfully by many companies.

- Keep all employment interview schedules running on time. Remind all those involved in the interviewing process of the importance of keeping interviews on time.

- Use a followup schedule to ensure that all candidates receive appropriate information on the status of open positions. See that candidates are contacted after an employment decision has been made.

While these strategies will impress older job candidates, they also will undoubtedly improve the image created for *all* job candidates.

Don't send a desperation message. Older workers want to work where they feel they are special, and where they feel they are valued. A message that implies "We'll take anyone" is counterproductive to recruitment efforts for older persons.

To avoid sounding desperate, employers may want to evaluate the frequency of recruitment communications, the placement of recruitment messages, and the wording of the message itself. Recruitment advertisements should appear no more than one time per quarter directed to the same audience in the same publication or activity. Employers with pressing employment needs should look to a variety of recruitment activities to attract workers. For example, instead of running a help-wanted advertisement week after week, place an ad in another section of the paper, display a poster at grocery stores and community centers, and initiate a direct-mail campaign. By using a diversity of methods, the message is not perceived to be as negative.

The wording of the ad itself can be changed to eliminate desperation signals. For example, classified ads that merely say "Help Wanted" tend to be perceived more negatively than advertisements that appeal to reader benefits. An ad that asks candidates, "Are you ready to make the most of your life?" will certainly capture the attention and interest of readers more than one that says, "File clerks needed." One employer found that qualified candidates could be enticed by the message "Take a step up with a job with us." Another employer advertised, "Place your name on our recruitment waiting list," when a recruitment waiting list didn't actually exist. However, with the powerful, positive positioning of this ad, it wasn't long before the employer did have a waiting list!

Collaborate to meet senior employment goals. Very few companies have much experience in attracting and retaining older workers. Companies have had more experience in looking for ways to move their older workers out to pasture. For those employers now interested in developing new strategies for attracting and retaining these workers, outside assistance may be needed.

Government-funded employment and training programs are available to help the employer train and place older adults. Older worker employment and training programs have expertise in dealing with older workers, and are typically most interested in working with employers to make the older worker connection.

Two government-funded programs that work with employees fifty-five and older are The Job Training Partnership Act (JTPA) and the Senior Community Service Employment Progam (SCSEP). The JTPA operates through local public/private partnerships called Private Industry Councils (PICs). The SCSEP operates through ten national sponsors and through government-operated and nonprofit agencies in each state and territory. The ten national sponsors include:

- National Council on the Aging

- National Urban League

- American Association of Retired Persons

- National Caucus and Center on Black Aged

- Green Thumb

- National Association for Hispanic Elderly

- National Council of Senior Citizens

- National Forest Service

- National Indian Council on Aging Inc.

- National Pacific/Asian Resource Center on Aging.

Additional contact information on these organizations can be found in the appendix, as well as information on services they provide to employers.

In working with government-funded programs, some guidelines for employers in building more effective relationships are as follows:

- Take the initiative and call the local office of one of the national programs, or contact the local Private Industry Council for information on what agency provides employment services to older adults.

- Make an appointment to talk with the program director or the program counselor to discuss specific employment needs and questions. Invite the program director to the employment site for a tour of the facility so that job specifications and accommodations can be addressed.

- Give feedback to organizations that provide older worker candidates for open positions. Be sure to explain to the program coordinator how the candidate was suited or unsuited for the position. In this way, the service organization will have a much clearer perspective on future openings and on determining which candidates will be more suited for those positions.

- Build relationships with service providers by offering to sponsor joint recruiting events. Many of these organizations have limited funds for outreach activities, and would enjoy the benefits of working with an employer and sharing recruiting costs. Many employers find that their credibility is enhanced in the recruitment of older workers when an older worker organization is cosponsoring the event.

- Maintain relationships with these organizations by providing ongoing feedback on the performance of older worker candidates who have been placed through the organization. Be sure to continue to notify the organization of current and future employment needs.

There can be many benefits for employers who work with employment and training programs:

- Assessment of candidates' skills and abilities.
- Screening of job candidates to ensure a job match.

- Job training for older candidates who do not possess requisite skills.

- Employability skills training for candidates who lack self-confidence.

Older candidates who work with these programs must meet certain eligibility requirements, which often means a financial need for work. Therefore, candidates who are referred through these programs have a strong interest in working.

Certain older worker organizations maintain listings of their client's skills, and publish these for employers. Check to see if the local programs offer this service.

Many employers have had some real successes in working with older worker organizations on joint recruitment activities. Some of the types of recruitment activities that could be cosponsored include:

- Career fairs/Job fairs

- Posters

- Information seminars

- Open houses

- Newspaper advertising

- Direct-mail campaigns

- Public service announcements

One employer found that a local television station that featured stories of interest to the general public was interested in a partnership developed by the employer and an older worker organization. An employer representative and the service organization representative were interviewed together, giving both the program and the employer valuable visibility in the community for future recruitment efforts.

While most organizations that serve older workers are most interested in working closely with employers, there are some issues to be aware of in dealing effectively with these groups. One is that most older worker organizations have income guidelines for their program participants. That is, they want to place their clients in positions that meet a certain standard salary level. In this way they ensure that their clients are placed in quality work environments—which is the ultimate goal of these programs. Therefore, the employer who is willing to pay only minimum wage will find that some government programs may be unwilling to actively work to place their clients with these employers, especially when there are other employers within the community willing to pay more.

Government-funded employment and training programs will also be wary of working with employers who are interested in large numbers of their clients. They may assume that the employer is not concerned with quality work experiences for their clients, and is only interested in finding bodies to fill positions. Employers who wish to work with these organizations should take the time to show the opportunities and benefits in employment with their companies.

In approaching older worker programs, indicate an interest in a long-term relationship, and in making successful placements one at a time. Too often employers' dreams of placing many older workers turn into failures if too much is attempted too soon. Service providers will appreciate the focus on making quality placements, and generally the employer will ultimately benefit from some initial successes on which to build.

Be competitive, and be prepared to sell the company's distinctive difference to older workers. Often, older persons who are considering reentering the work force, or who are investigating a second or third career, may be hesitant, like the window shopper described earlier. Many may feel they are being discriminated against, or may not be confident of their abilities in the new career. At any rate, most older people are not actively seeking employment, and therefore must be sold on the idea.

Every employer has something distinctive to offer employees, and should evaluate what can be offered that is attractive to older persons. For example, one employer may be able to offer job-sharing for technical and professional positions, which may attract older persons who are interested in working part time in the professional capacity they held in their first career. Specifying this opportunity in the recruitment message will attract many older people. Another employer, however, may be able to offer a variety of temporary positions that employees can fill when they want to work. Again, by advertising this information, you can attract many older persons.

Employers will do well to analyze the variety of selling opportunities they possess. Some of the features, advantages, and benefits for employment may be developed by investigating the following topics:

- Parent company

- Size of organization

- Years in business

- Quality of the product/service

- Culture of the organization

- Management style

- Company goals

- Salary and benefits

- Training and development programs

- Performance evaluations
- Incentives and rewards
- Job design
- Departmental goals, leadership
- Internal communications

While this is only a partial list, it should help employers identify areas in which there are some "selling" opportunities. Recruitment messages should take advantage of as many of these assets as possible.

Companies also can benefit from developing a sales presentation for the interviewing process. As many older workers will be increasingly sought after by more and more employers, these employers will need to present their organizations in the most favorable way possible. All of those involved in the employment process should be trained in ways not only to sell the organization but to sell it to older workers in particular.

Be imaginative and creative in planning recruitment activities for older workers. Innovative and nontraditional methods are being used by employers in attracting older workers back into the workplace. Some of these ideas are addressed next.

Newspapers and magazines. While the help-wanted section of the newspaper is one of the more commonly used places to recruit older workers, it can also be one of the least effective, since many older people are not actively seeking employment and are not looking in the help-wanted or classified section of the newspaper. However, older worker candidates often can be attracted by placing recruitment advertisements in alternate sections of the paper, such as the television section, which many older people read each day. Another good place is near the obituary section! It makes sense, doesn't it, to place ads where the older adult is reading the paper each day? Another excellent section of the paper is near the grocery store ads on coupon days, since this section also has a large older readership.

Alternative papers can also be effective for recruiting older workers. Local, community, ethnic, and church newspapers can be excellent ways to reach a specific market.

Church bulletins and newsletters, club publications and magazines, convenience store "bargain" shoppers, and free television guides can be low-cost and effective in reaching certain older worker populations.

Magazines that reach the senior market can also be effective. However, this method can be very costly. For example, *Modern Maturity,* AARP's magazine, now costs $171,000 per page in advertising costs! The reason for this high cost is the high readership of the magazine—it is number two, second only to *Reader's Digest.*[3]

Open houses. An open house is an event sponsored by an organization either at the employer's place of business or at a community center or hotel. Older workers can be attracted by making it a fun event—why not consider an "unretirement" party? Offer something free, either refreshments, information, or other giveaways.

Open houses are excellent for attracting career shifters—those who have never worked within the industry or occupation before. An open house gives these individuals a chance to "check out" what the position and company has to offer, without feeling compelled to commit to an employment interview.

Employers should offer recruitment literature, and should have ample staff to mingle with the participants and to answer questions and address concerns one-on-one. Formal interviews can be scheduled on the premises or within the next week. Employers can also take the opportunity to followup with candidates with borderline interest in the next month or even in the next year.

Information seminars. Older individuals want and need information on health concerns, financial issues, and housing matters, as well as employment options. Advertise and conduct an information seminar that offers a variety of topics to older adults, including some specific benefits of a second career with the organization.

Television. While advertising on prime-time television can be out of the budget for most employers, it can be quite affordable—sometimes free—through public service announcements (PSAs). Employers should check with their local stations to see if such announcements are available at no cost.

Cable television is also gaining in popularity, and many local cable stations offer "bulletin board" advertising at very reasonable rates. Call the local cable television station for rate and viewer information.

Direct mail. By using "age selects" the older worker candidate can be targeted in direct mail. Direct mail is an excellent choice for recruitment, since seniors are two times as likely to buy products based upon direct-mail solicitation.[4] Older people can also be segmented by many other subsets, including income levels, educational levels, geographic location, occupation, or past occupation.

Because this method is so targeted, it can be extremely effective. For example, one employer was interested in identifying older women within one ZIP code who might be interested in temporary secretarial and clerical work. By using direct mail, a mailing list was identified that could segment women who lived within the ZIP code desired, who had previously worked in secretarial and clerical positions, and who were over fifty years of age. A letter was developed that spoke to these women's desires for part-time and temporary work that would permit them to add to their income without jeopardizing Social Security benefits, and that would allow them to meet and interact with others. The mailing was a tremendous success.

Because of the ability of the employer to define the targeted population, direct-mail campaigns can be used to target candidates for a wide range of positions, from technical and professional to sales to clerical.

Direct-mail campaigns are usually low in cost, with many mailing lists available for purchase anywhere from thirty dollars to one hundred dollars per thousand names secured, usually with a minimum cost of three hundred dollars. Add the cost of postage and the mailing piece, which is sent to only those persons who meet the specifications for the job, and the total costs are quite nominal when compared to the cost of an ad in the help-wanted section of the newspaper.

Operation Able of Greater Boston has had excellent results with direct mail. By using what the organization calls a "blitz" model, the campaign receives short-term high visibility and media involvement. For best success, the organization coupled direct mail with a strong media campaign. Older adults were invited through the variety of messages to a meeting where more information was offered on employment opportunities.[5]

Mass transit. By placing recruiting messages inside or outside public transportation, the message reaches many older individuals who need to work. They may, however, have no transportation of their own, so will need to work where public transportation is accessible.

The most successful mass-transit messages are those that are placed inside a bus, train, or subway, and that include a tear-off mini-application form. In this way the candidate has contact information available on the form, and can easily follow up with the employer. By using this kind of response form, employers are also able to better track the response rates to determine effectiveness of this advertising.

Posters. Posters can reach a large number of older individuals in places they visit every day. Consider post offices, grocery stores, banks, community centers, medical buildings, senior centers, libraries, laundromats, churches, and drug stores, as these locations often have community bulletin boards. Attach a mini-application that includes contact information. Some employers have used posters without tear-off application blanks, only to find that interested candidates remove the entire poster so that they will have the name and number of the employer to contact later.

Referral programs/task forces. Asking for referrals from older workers is probably one of the best methods of finding interested older worker candidates. Often, current employees are the best recruiters, especially when they are happy with their employer. Employees typically will recommend candidates with the same attitudes toward work, knowing that if they refer someone who is inefficient, they will have to work even harder. Older workers, with their traditional strong work ethic, will want to retain their good standing with the employer, and tend to refer excellent candidates.

By offering an incentive to employees who refer a candidate who is hired, employees are more likely to get involved with the referral system. Incentives can be cash, prizes, or other rewards. Value of the incentive should be commensurate with the level of the position being filled, the difficulty in hiring for that position, and the numbers of candidates needed for open positions. Employers often establish incentive amounts based upon the average cost per hire. The cost per hire is determined by adding all dollars spent on recruitment activities, and dividing by the number of candidates hired.

Employers also benefit from developing task forces of older workers to assist in creating strategies to recruit and retain more older workers. Kentucky Fried Chicken Corporation, for example, created a task force of older workers including management and hourly employees. Some mistakes were discovered, as well as some opportunities. One task force member pointed out that the company was spending too much time recruiting in a retirement community in which the residents had no real interest in work. The task force members then pointed out a mobile home park, in which there were many older persons who really needed some additional income. By listening to these older workers, the company was able to refocus its recruitment efforts and concentrate on activities that were more likely to produce results.

Other companies that have benefited from older worker task forces are Days Inn and Busch Gardens theme park in Williamsburg, Virginia. By asking their older employees about the best ways to recruit other older workers, these employers were able to attract candidates through newspaper, radio, flyers, and word of mouth.[6]

A quotation by Bert Kruger Smith sums up why older worker task forces can be important to the employer in developing effective recruiting messages and activities: "Everyone has been a child. All can understand through muffled memory how childhood was. But none has been old except those who are that now." Indeed, employers may look back and develop strategies for attracting young workers based upon their own personal experiences as a young person facing the world of work. However, it is impossible to project what it is like to be an older person investigating the prospects of working. By using the ideas and suggestions of older workers, employers are better able to develop strategies that reach out and speak to other older people.

Recruitment literature. Older adults like print messages; studies have shown it is the preferred medium with the mature market. These individuals want something they can take home and study.[7] Ad copy should be conversational and targeted to the older reader. Studies have shown that they like: relevant bits and pieces, nonabrasive, straightforward approaches, and credible, relevant endorsements.[8]

Typeface in recruiting materials should be serif style, not sans serif, as older eyes read this bookish style easier.[9] Keep print size a bit larger than usual, at least twelve points.

Use recruitment literature at open houses and career fairs, in one-on-one interviews, at presentations at clubs and organizations, and in direct-mail campaigns.

Job fairs. Job fairs can be an effective way to attract older individuals. By joining with other employers, or by participating in a job fair conducted by an outside agency, employers can target the older worker candidate. Government-funded employment and training programs working with older workers often sponsor such events; call local agencies to determine dates and locations.

When participating in job fairs, employers should ensure that their booth is competitive. Brochures and recruitment literature need to speak to the older candidate, either through targeted materials or by including older workers in recruitment pictures. Older worker candidates often are attracted to job fair booths, as are other candidates, by giveaways or prizes. Prizes should be items that will be valued by older persons. More older persons can be attracted to the booth by having candidates complete an information sheet or card, with the prize going to the person whose name is drawn. In this way, valuable contact information is secured for followup correspondence, or for later mailings.

Days Inn has had excellent results in using job fairs to staff many positions at its headquarters in Atlanta, Georgia. By using current older employees as "Star Recruiters," the company has doubled the number of older workers it employs. "Star Recruiters" attend the job fair to discuss positions at Days Inn, answer questions, and let other seniors know of the company's interest in hiring more older workers.[10] At a recent fair, the company added twenty older workers on the spot, with sixty-eight hires over the next three months.[11]

In New York City, the Department of Aging has hosted an annual "Ability is Ageless" job fair. With cosponsors WNBC-TV and the New York Chamber of Commerce, the event has attracted more than one hundred employers and four thousand older job seekers. The cost to employers was four hundred dollars; two hundred dollars for nonprofit organizations. One hospital hired four seniors on the spot for hard-to-fill positions. A retail chain said it saved ten thousand dollars by participating.[12]

Radio. Radio is an excellent medium for recruitment messages to older individuals, because older persons tend to listen to certain stations. Radio reaches 95 percent of the fifty-plus market each week. Studies have revealed that mature listeners tune in between 6:00 A.M. and 6:00 P.M.; early morning hours are best. Contact radio stations directly for listener demographic information, or call a recruitment advertising agency for this information. Typically, easy listening of the 1940s and 1950s, news, talk shows, classical, and adult contemporary are the best formats.[13]

Radio is best used for recruitment when a print ad is used with the message. For example, run radio messages in combination with an ad in Sunday's paper, and make sure the radio ad specifically mentions that more detailed information can be found in Sunday's classified section (or wherever the ad may appear). Radio is often used successfully with print to advertise open houses and career and job fairs.

Networking. Some of the most successful campaigns to recruit older workers have used old-fashioned networking. By letting people in the community know, officially and unofficially, about their desire to recruit more older workers, many employers have been able to attract these workers. Spread the word through churches, community groups, agencies, and other older workers. Kiwanis Clubs, Rotary Clubs, and Lions Clubs can be helpful. AARP's Work Equity Department recommends using seniors to make these presentations whenever possible.[14]

Telemarketing. Reaching older worker candidates by phone can be another effective way to recruit. Employers can obtain phone numbers by using directories (church, community centers, clubs) and mailing lists. Older persons should be used as callers whenever possible to strengthen the "testimonial" appeal. Vermont Associates for Training and Development feels that the personality of the caller is key. The caller should be upbeat, friendly, low-key, and skilled at conversation. To ensure success, the organization has a script to recruit older workers.[15]

Door hangers. Messages on door hangers can attract individuals within a specific geographic area. Product messages that may appeal to an older consumer, together with a recruiting message, can be an excellent combination.

Recruiting vans. Some employers have found that when the candidates don't come to them, they need to go to the candidates. This is particularly true with older people who are not actively seeking employment; the employer must make the recruitment opportunity highly accessible to the candidate. By buying or leasing a van, employers can take a staffing office "on wheels" to areas where there are older candidates. Grocery stores on coupon days, banks and post offices the first of the month, churches, community centers, and laundromats are excellent places to park a mobile recruiting unit. Since some shopping centers have restrictions on these vehicles and their signs, be sure to gain clearance from the proper authorities. Advertise about the appearance of these vans through flyers, door hangers, posters, and radio and newspaper notices.

Lease a van in which applications can be completed and interviews can be conducted. By making it easy for the older candidate to investigate the employment opportunity in a convenient location, the employer is more likely to recruit the candidate who is not actively seeking work.

Point-of-sale. Retailers have an opportunity to recruit their older consumers when these individuals come into the establishment. Use point-of-sale recruitment messages on cash register tapes, bag stuffers, table tents, posters, counter cards, banners, reader board signs, tray liners, customer billings, and literature. Some employers are even including recruitment messages on the telephone when customers and others make calls to the company and are placed on hold. Mervin's department stores, headquartered in Hayward, California, successfully use bag stuffers that depict older employees.[16]

Inviting back retirees. For many employers, there is a wonderful resource of skilled, experienced, mature individuals right in their own back yard. By inviting previous employees to come back to work, many employers *and* their retired employees are benefiting.

Consider the example of Varian Associates, a $1-billion-a-year high-tech equipment manufacturer that desperately needed the skills of a retiree—Bill Ames, a rare employee who knew the process for testing a Klystron microwave tube. All the company had to do was ask, and offer Ames a part-time schedule that met his needs.[17]

High-visibility event. "Hire the Older Worker Week" is the second week in March each year, and provides employers an opportunity to plan an event that will focus on the employment of older workers.[18] A conference, career fair, open house, or "unretirement" party could be the focus for an event that would invite older adults to investigate employment opportunities, while at the same time making the community aware of these activities.

By using a variety of creative and imaginative strategies, employers will fare much better in competing in the recruiting wars for their fair share of older workers.

Use a variety of recruitment messages and activities. An assortment of recruitment messages and activities can be used to attract older workers. By relying on several strategies, employers will find that their recruitment needs are more easily met. Further, by limiting overuse of one strategy, employers avoid the desperation message of too-frequent communications, providing for better recruitment outcomes.

Be persistent. Because the older candidate is an elusive candidate, many employers have become discouraged in their recruitment efforts. However, employers who are diligent in their recruiting are having excellent results in terms of the payoffs in this initial investment of time and money.

Selecting Older Workers

Once an employer takes steps to recruit older worker candidates, how can the employer make the best selection decisions?

Employee Standards

One of the biggest mistakes organizations make in selecting older workers is in concluding that all older workers are superior candidates for all positions, which is, of course, incorrect. While many older workers are excellent candidates for many positions, they are still individuals, with strengths and weaknesses that make them more or less suited for a variety of positions.

Employers have also made mistakes in hiring older workers when they lower their employment standards and expect less of older workers than they do of other workers. While it is commendable for employers to try to accommodate workers' individual differences, it is usually disastrous to have a different set of expectations for older workers than for other workers. Double standards invariably lead to resentment by other employees, confused supervisory personnel, and lower morale. Older workers themselves may be demoralized. The best strategy is in uniformity of performance expectations, with the only accommodations being those for slight modifications to the physical work setting, if necessary.

Age Discrimination

What questions can an employer legally ask an older worker? Are there any questions that would be asked of an older worker that would not be asked of a younger worker? Is there any question that would be asked of a younger person that would not be asked of an older person?

It is illegal to ask any questions, directly or indirectly, that would determine the age of the applicant. Questions such as "How old are you?" or "What year were you born?" are illegal, as well as those questions that indirectly ask the question, such as, "What year did you graduate from high school/college?"

Generally, any question that might be asked of an older candidate should be asked appropriately of a younger candidate, and vice versa. In fact, this is usually a good method to determine the appropriateness of a question. However, some questions will need to be tailored to the job candidate. For example, while it is always appropriate to ask all job candidates about their most recent work experiences, it would not be appropriate to ask older job candidates about their first jobs out of school or their experiences in school. Keep employment questions focused in the recent past.

Some employers may also have concern for older candidates' abilities to handle physical activity, such as heavy lifting, bending, or standing for long periods of time. If these are requirements for all candidates working in the position, then the question of physical ability should be raised with all candidates, not just older workers. When a question like this is raised *only* with older worker candidates, and not all candidates, it can be considered discriminatory.

Assistance

In many cases, government-funded employment and training programs are willing to help employers provide in-depth assessment that will result in more successful placement. These programs can also assist older adults, who may lack self-confidence after an absence from the work force, in presenting themselves in a positive, assertive manner in the interviewing process.

Conclusion

Organizations interested in attracting and selecting older workers can use a variety of traditional and nontraditional strategies in targeting this labor market segment. Employers need to recognize the challenge in developing recruitment activities and messages that speak specifically to older adults, in places they frequent in the course of their daily activities. To select the best, companies need to ensure that discriminatory practices are eliminated, and that all candidates—especially older worker candidates—have an opportunity to be matched with the right job.

Notes

1. See "Selling to the Age Wave," *Selling to Seniors*, June 1988, p. 1.
2. See *How to Recruit Older Workers*, Worker Equity Department, American Association of Retired Persons, 1988, p. 6.
3. See "Magazines Reach for the Mature Market," *Selling to Seniors*, August 1988, p. 1.
4. See "Applying the Rules of Marketing to Elders," *Selling to Seniors*, June 1988, p. 3.
5. See Pat Elmer, Robin Battista, "Innovations in Recruitment," *Making JTPA Work for Older Persons: A National Catalogue of Practical How-To's*, National Association of State Units on Aging, May 1987, pp. 71–72.
6. See "Theme Park Recruits Older Workers by Stressing Opportunity to Make Friends," *The Older Worker*, September 1988, p. 4.
7. See "Heterogeneous Mature Market Spawns A Variety of Tips on How to Reach Them," *Selling to Seniors*, October 1988, p. 3.
8. See "Study Seniors Experience to Understand Their Values, Ad Agency Official Suggests," *Selling to Seniors*, October 1988, p. 1–2.
9. See "Using Direct Mail, Advertising Agencies," *Selling to Seniors*, August 1988, p. 8.
10. See Linda Fernandez, *Now Hiring*, BNA Publishing, 1989, p. 119.
11. See "Older Worker Job Fairs Prove Successful Recruitment Techniques, Days Inn Finds," *The Older Worker*, August 1988, p. 1.
12. See "Citywide Fair Attracts 4,000 Older Job-Seekers, More Than 100 Businesses," *The Older Worker*, November 1988, p. 4.
13. See "Statistics Show That Radio is One of the Best Ways to Reach the Senior Market," *Selling to Seniors*, May 1988, p. 1.
14. See *How to Recruit Older Workers*, Worker Equity Department, American Association of Retired Persons, 1988, p. 6.

15. See Pat Elmer, Robin Battista, "Innovations in Recruitment," *Making JTPA Work for Older Persons: A National Catalogue of Practical How-To's*, National Association of State Units on Aging, May 1987, pp. 71–72.
16. See "Mervin's Stores Seeks Mature Part-Timers," *The Older Worker*, July 1988, p. 1.
17. See Anthony Ramírez, "Making Better Use of Older Workers," *Fortune*, January 30, 1989, p. 179.
18. See "How to Get Your Recruitment Message Out," *The Older Worker*, May 1988, pp. 2–3.

4
Teaching New Tricks: Training and Retraining the Older Worker

Old age and the test of time teach many things.

—Sophocles

A s the country grows older, it grows wiser, because time is a valuable teacher. However, when it comes to job-specific skills, employers cannot sit back and hope older workers either mysteriously absorb these skills from the environment or go on to retirement. Too often today, employers are not investing in the company's future by offering job training and retraining opportunities to their older workers.

Smart employers are beginning to realize that in an environment in which job skills are quickly becoming obsolete, care must be taken to ensure that all workers are brought up-to-date. One study by a California-based think tank revealed that workers in the year 2020 will need to be retrained up to thirteen times to keep pace with technological changes in the work environment.

Business leaders are alarmed at the numbers of workers who are functionally and marginally illiterate, and therefore are unable to learn new job skills. New workers often do not possess the job skills needed in today's work world.

Further, with the baby bust generation now entering the employment ranks in increasingly small numbers, employers who need technically and professionally trained employees are learning that the older worker is a valuable commodity indeed. Employers know that to remain competitive and to be effective in meeting staffing needs, older workers must be retained and retrained. Additionally, older workers must be attracted, oriented, and trained for new positions, as the dwindling number of teenagers results in labor shortages.

Older workers are not the only ones needing new training. Supervisors managing a highly diverse work force for the first time also require training in ways to better manage and retain this dynamic work force.

Some of the major issues facing employers in dealing with training and retraining for older workers are:

- How does orientation differ for older workers?

- What is "pretraining" and how does it apply to older workers?

- What are the basic principles in adult learning and how do they apply to older workers?

- How does training differ for older adults?

- How do instructors need to change their methodologies in dealing with older learners?

- What are the issues in teaching older workers new high-tech skills?

- What assessment tools are appropriate for older workers?

- What are the developmental issues in training for older workers currently in the work force?

- What training tools are needed by supervisors who are now responsible for managing a highly diverse work force?

- What training assistance is available to employers?

This chapter deals with these subjects, and offers suggestions to companies that are facing these new dilemmas of the 1990s.

Orienting the New Older Worker to the Job

Older workers new to the job are typically less confident and more unsure about their employment decision than are their younger counterparts. They often see themselves as different from their younger counterparts, and see the new employment arena as quite different from their last job, reports Greg Newton, President of Newton & Associates. Newton points out that nontraditional workers most want the orientation session to be a chance to build relationships and to bond with the organization. Newton reports that these are some of the common mistakes made by employers:

- The orientation is seen as a single, one-day event, as opposed to a longer-term process.

- The orientation forces too much information too quickly onto new employees, making them feel inadequate and incompetent.

- The orientation often focuses on what not to do, instead of what to do, mistakes instead of achievements, and information rather than relationships.

- Orientations do not focus on making the new employee feel at home in the new organization, and part of the "family."

- The organization is not ready for the new employee. This can mean anything from not having the office and supplies ready to not having scheduled someone to provide initial training.

- The organization does not let new employees know they are important, and that the company cares about the new employee as a person.

- Few resources, either in staff or in dollars, are allocated to a professional presentation to new employees in order to overcome "buyer's remorse."

Buyer's remorse occurs after a major purchase is made, when the buyer begins to wonder if a good purchase decision was made. "Did I spend too much?" "Is this a good value?" "Did I do the right thing?" These are questions that indicate buyer's remorse, and are similar to the questions that many new employees, particularly older workers, ask once they have accepted a new position. "How will I fit in on the new job?" "Am I too old for this job?" "Can I be successful in this position?" Employers need to establish an orientation process that will help new employees, especially older ones, overcome this phenomenon.

Pretraining

Today, many companies find that job candidates do not possess the job skills necessary for open positions. One alternative is to hire individuals who do not possess the requisite skills and provide on-the-job training to bring them up to minimum standards. Another alternative is to offer pretraining to job candidates.

Pretraining describes training provided to job candidates before a job offer is extended. Individuals who are interested in employment with an organization can enroll in free classes that teach basic skills particular to the job. Once candidates successfully complete the pretraining and pass a test, thus signifying mastery of the subject matter, they are guaranteed a job with that company. This process is gaining popularity with high-technology companies, in particular, because fewer job candidates possess the level of skills needed in the work environment.

This pretraining concept is being used specifically with older workers by Senior Employment Resources, a non-profit, no-fee employment agency in northern Virginia that serves people over age fifty-five. This agency found that many of its older job seekers lacked the necessary skills for good jobs, but were unable to finance skill training, or were afraid of the training process.

To develop the needed skills, Senior Employment Services (SES) created Senior Communications Services (SCS), an organization of seniors who have communications backgrounds and who want to remain active in occupations such as editing, writing, publishing, and graphic arts. SES and SCS work together to provide pretraining services to older adults. Pretraining opportunities are on high-tech equipment, such as computers, word processors, printers, and graphics equipment, and involve one-on-one tutoring. Through this process, older adults are able to overcome their fears of learning and of technology, and are better able to secure positions in the fields of publishing or graphics.[1]

Adult Learning Principles Revisited

To effectively train older workers, it is important to review the adult learning principles, and then to analyze what the differences are in training older workers as opposed to younger workers. The basic laws of adult learning are the Law of Effect, the Law of Exercise, the Law of Readiness, the Law of Association, and the Law of Primacy.

The Law of Effect

Adults learn best when they are in pleasant surroundings—
a friendly, supportive environment. Because adults tend to
take correction personally, they are more comfortable in an
environment in which mistakes are accepted and corrected
in a positive, nonconfrontational manner. Adults tend to
learn best in smaller groups, or in one-on-one sessions,
because they feel they can make a mistake without losing
face with a lot of people watching.

The Law of Exercise

Adults learn best when they have the opportunity to try out
what they have learned. By demonstrating their knowledge
through practice, adults effectively learn new tasks. Practice
makes perfect. Adults can practice what they've learned
through case studies, simulation games, small-group discussions, written exercises, role play, and question-and-answer
periods.

The Law of Readiness

When adults know the "why" behind learning, they are
more open and receptive to new ideas. Adults must see
how they will apply the knowledge; once they do, they are
more apt to learn. This is why many organizations are
having success in teaching literacy skills to adults; they find
that when adults are shown *how* this skill can help them
prepare meals by reading recipes, write letters to friends,
read the weather report, or interpret a checking account
statement, adults learn quickly and readily.

The Law of Association

Adults learn best when they can apply what they are learning to past experiences. They do well when they learn

"building-block" style, and add new knowledge to previous knowledge. Instructors of adult students find that by first reviewing what the students already know, they can build effectively on this knowledge and teach new ideas and principles.

The Law of Primacy

Adults retain most effectively information that was learned first. Because of this, teachers should limit the number of new ideas presented in any given period of time. Some trainers feel that even sophisticated adults can handle only about four or five new ideas within a twenty-minute period.[2] Key points should be clearly emphasized.

These adult learning principles point to the fact that adults should be trained differently from children. They want to be treated as adults, with instructors acknowledging their past learning. Adults are independent people who are in charge of their lives, and they should be treated as such. They also want to be able to understand how new learning fits into their lives, and how they will use this knowledge.

Differences in Learning

There are many more similarities than differences in training older adults versus younger adults. All the principles of adult learning certainly apply to older adults: they want a supportive, friendly environment; they want to be able to apply what they have learned; they want to know why they are learning what they are being taught; they want to build new learning on past experiences.

What are the specific differences in training adults? How should businesses change to meet the learning needs of older employees? Key differences in training the older adult learner are described next.

Older adults can take up to two times as long to learn a new task or skill. Just as all people learn at different rates of speed, older adults learn at different rates. For many older adults, however, it can take up to two times as long to learn new information because of the way the brain changes as aging occurs. While some businesses are concerned with this difference, it can be argued that the additional training investment is easily recouped when the longer length of service of older workers is considered. Further, once older workers learn a new task, they tend to perform that task with fewer mistakes than their younger counterparts.

Older adults perceive light differently as they age. As people age, their vision changes. In particular, the way in which the eye receives light changes. Because of this, some training materials can be difficult for the older adult to read. Glossy materials are difficult to see, as are low-contrast colors, such as blues and greens and pastels.

Older adults often do not see or hear as clearly as younger adults. Because vision and hearing often deteriorate as the aging process occurs, many older adults are not as adept at reading small print or hearing soft, high-pitched sounds.

Older adults can take longer to store and retrieve data. Because of the changes to the brain in the aging process, it can take some older adults longer to store and retrieve data, slowing down the learning process as well as recall. For most older adults, however, mental functioning is seldom affected until age seventy.

Older adults are often unfamiliar with high-technology terminology and equipment. Because some older adults have been out of the work force, or have not participated in training on computers and other high-tech equipment, they tend to be more unfamiliar with terminology and skills that relate to this technology. While many older workers have fears concerning their ability to learn in this area, there is no information to support the premise that older adults are unable to learn these new skills.

Adapting the Training Process

To adapt the training process for older learners, businesses should make the following changes.

Allow self-paced learning. Since all adults tend to learn at differing rates of speed, and especially since older adults may take longer to learn new skills, a self-paced training system makes sense not just for older workers, but for all workers. When workers learn at their own pace they build self-esteem and self-confidence.

Use training materials with high-contrast colors and bold typeface. By using easy-to-read training materials, employers make learning more effective. Eliminate high-gloss items, particularly laminated pages or posters, as these are also difficult for all workers to see clearly.

Avoid posting training materials above eye level. Because many older adults wear bifocals, looking up to read a training poster can be difficult. Keep all postings that include employee information at eye level.

Speak clearly and distinctly during training sessions. Instructors should use good diction, speaking clearly at a
natural rate of speed. Hearing-impaired people should sit at
the front of the room so the speaker's face can be clearly
seen. Remove distracting sounds that may interfere with
listening.

*Use adult learning principles to train older adults on new
skills.* Because it can take longer for older adults to store
and retrieve data, it makes sense to break down all skills
into small tasks, and then build upon that knowledge. A
modularized training program helps all learners use a
building-block approach to facilitate the learning process.
Not only is a modular training program effective in providing a building-block approach, but it also facilitates many
older workers' desires for part-time work. Shorter training
segments enable workers to exercise a more flexible schedule without falling behind in the training.

   Also, emphasize key learning points, and don't try to
teach too much too quickly. Especially in teaching computer and other high-tech skills, use a self-paced approach
to help those learners who are more unfamiliar with the
process.

Instructors Need New Methodologies

Other modifications to facilitate learning for older adults
should include the following strategies.

*Provide a friendly, supportive environment when training
older adults.* Even though all workers learn best when the
training environment is warm and supportive, older adults
are often more fearful and lacking in self-confidence. Many
older adults are afraid of losing face, and of appearing

dumb to their co-workers. Also, many older workers may be entering the work force for the first time, for example, displaced homemakers, or may be reentering the workplace after a lengthy absence. By providing a caring, supportive environment, older workers not only will learn more quickly, but will be retained in the work force more effectively.

Eliminate jargon from the workplace, or at least explain it from the start. Jargon is commonplace. One company manager said all the company's acronyms had finally been captured in a dictionary, but even the dictionary was given an acronym! Jargon, including the use of acronyms, tends to form barriers between "those who know" and "those who don't know." Jargon tends to perpetuate a we–they mentality, and while this can be powerful in building company allegiance and team affiliation, this mentality can place walls between new employees and the rest of the organization. Especially with new older workers who already may feel different from other employees, eliminating any barriers is important in creating a positive learning environment, as well as enhancing employee retention. Smart businesses will ensure that a class on company and industry jargon is covered on the first day of the job.

Use multiple training methodologies in teaching older adults. While all adults tend to learn best when they are exposed to a variety of training methods—lecture, group discussion, case studies, individual exercises, video, demonstration—older workers find they benefit more from certain mediums. Older adults tend to place more credibility on the printed word, and will benefit from seeing training information in print. Further, instructors of older workers report that these learners are more likely to want to take work home to study and review. Printed materials permit this learning to take place.

There also has been some discussion among trainers of older adults regarding the effectiveness of video training. Most conclude that video training is effective with older adults, especially after they become familiar with the operation of the video equipment. Often, the only barrier to video learning for older adults is lack of familiarity with the tape player.

Use older workers to teach other older adults. Older workers report that they feel more comfortable in the learning environment when the instructor is an older adult. Often, older instructors are more sensitive to adult learning differences, and can adapt the learning environment to meet the needs of the older worker. Further, many older learners feel with another older worker as their instructor that "If they can do it, I can do it," thus bolstering confidence and self-esteem.

Group older workers in the learning process. Older workers like to work side by side with their peers. In this congenial learning environment, adult learners are more apt to learn new tasks effectively. Also, by seeing other workers who are "just like me," older adults find that their self-confidence is enhanced. Involve other older workers in the learning process as much as possible.

Build upon valuable life experiences. Older learners have valuable life and work experiences that should not be ignored by instructors. By building upon older adults' experiences, learning and self-esteem are enhanced.

Link learning with rewards. Let older workers know that the information and skills they learn will have a direct impact on rewards and incentives with their job. For example, if completing a training module makes the older employee eligible for a pay increase, be certain that this information is made clear to the worker.

Teaching High-technology Skills

There has been a general fear on the part of businesses consistent with the maxim "You can't teach an old dog new tricks"; businesses are afraid older workers may not be able to learn the skills involved in computers and computer technology. While some older adults have these same fears, there is a lot of evidence to the contrary.

The Travelers, known for its efforts in recruiting and "unretiring" its retirees, has been very successful in training older workers in computer skills. Travelers has offered paid computer training to those employees in the company's Retiree Job Bank who have keyboard experience. A majority of older workers have already indicated an interest in learning these skills.

One program, funded by the Private Industry Council in Portland, Oregon is having great success in training older adults in computer skills. The program, called New Directions, is offered to unemployed persons fifty-five and over. The training period is for six hours a day, three days a week, for eight weeks.

One reason for this program's success is that it starts with the very basics, reports Karen Quitt, program coordinator. She says many programs fail in teaching older adults these skills because the instructors assume a skill and knowledge level that just doesn't exist with many older adults. She also says that even though instructors must start with basics, they cannot ignore the fact that *adults* are being taught; instruction cannot be condescending. Quitt reports that once the older adults become involved in the learning process, they learn just as quickly as any other group that doesn't have basic knowledge about computers.[3]

Another innovative approach to teaching computer skills to older adults is a computer club in Louisville, Kentucky. The Silver Fox Computer Club is for adults who are fifty-plus, offering more than forty classes a week in more than twenty software packages.

Club participants have a variety of motivations for attending. Some come because they are interested in purchasing a computer and the classes give them valuable information on what they should buy. Others attend because they feel left out at work, and want to gain the skills that will ensure a job for their future. Others want to learn, but are afraid of losing face at work, and use this club as an opportunity to be just as competent as the younger workers when computer training is offered at work.

Pat Breathitt, co-owner of the club, which is a subsidiary of Business Computers and Software II, reports that the club's success is largely attributed to the fact that their training is tailored to older adults. She says older adults, like herself, have no less ability, but approach learning a little differently. She hires older instructors for this reason.

The Silver Fox Computer Club instructor and coordinator, Allys Huff, says there are a few modifications that instructors must make in successful training technology to older adults. She advises:

- Don't do things for them. Let older adults do it for themselves. She said there is a real temptation to press buttons for them, as they tend to be a little slower. Exert patience, and let them progress at their own pace.

- Keep the training process slow and simple. Repeat instructions and have learners repeat their actions.

- Give older learners something in writing, as it helps to

reinforce learning. Often they take instructional materials home with them.

Breathitt says classes are intentionally kept small, with no more than twelve people per class. Also, each class is one hour long, with each module running for four weeks. This schedule is compatible with older adults' schedules, and helps them feel comfortable in repeating a module if they still don't feel they have mastered that portion of the material.

Breathitt says one of the greatest things about The Silver Fox Computer Club is the excitement and enthusiasm of its students. "When students finish a class here, they really feel so good about themselves," she says.[4]

One restaurant company reported good results in training its older workers to use electronic cash registers. Initially the training manager complained that older trainees had difficulty learning to operate the new cash registers, and seemed to be afraid of breaking or jamming the registers in some way. The company overcame this problem by introducing a game to their older trainees: if anyone jammed the cash register during training, they would receive a twenty-five-dollar reward! This game eased the stress, and made the learning process more effective. Very few rewards were ever paid out!

While many organizations may be concerned about technology training for their older workers, experiences have demonstrated that when the needs and concerns of the older trainees are met, older adults learn and adapt quickly to high-technology concepts. There is a place for older workers in this age of advancing technology.

Assessing the Older Worker

Assessment is an important tool in training and development, as it permits an analysis of the strengths and weaknesses of employees so that further training can be developed, jobs can be redesigned, and career planning can be enhanced. Assessment determines the path that employees will take, as well as the training that will be provided. For older workers, the assessment process becomes critical in proper placement, training, retraining, and development.

Assessment programs for older adults should include a variety of components:[5]

Work and Training History

An inventory of work experiences should include detailed information concerning job titles, responsibilities, accomplishments, and abilities. Training courses attended should be included on this listing. This information can be obtained from employee records, but should be augmented with a comprehensive information interview that includes the employee's perceptions of strengths, weaknesses, and barriers to employment goals.

Educational Status Survey

Transcripts should be obtained, as well as tests and interview evaluation forms, to assess current competency levels.

Life Experience Evaluation

Unpaid work experiences should be included on assessment questionnaires, including volunteer work, home duties, accomplishments, and all transferable skills.

Informal/Formal Interest and Skills Inventories

Tests and other assessment tools can measure job-related interests, aptitudes, and abilities, and can be excellent indicators of job potential as well as specific employee needs, including flex-scheduling and other job requirements. Self-assessment checklists can permit employees to explore personal characteristics and preferences for work. Aptitude tests, such as the U.S. Department of Labor's General Aptitude Test Battery (GATB), can assess general learning abilities, as well as other specific abilities. The test is available through the local employment service.

Employment Planning and Goal Setting

The final step in the assessment process is determining employee career goals and objectives and charting a plan to achieve those goals. Vocational interviews provide feedback to employees, as well as a formal time period in which to chart future training for current and future job responsibilities.

How Assessment Is Different For Older Adults

Formal test results should be tempered with informal measures and other assessment methods, because many older adults do not perform well on tests. Some of the reasons for this lower scoring are lower educational attainment, unfamiliarity with testing procedures, or test anxiety.[6] Everything possible should be done to lessen testing anxiety; retesting should not be overlooked as a means to obtain valid test results.

Since some older workers suffer from low self-confidence, the assessment process should be as positive and supportive as possible. Assessment interviews should be designed to focus on strengths, and should give positive, constructive feedback on developmental issues. When properly administered, the assessment process can be an effective tool in career training and development.

Physical Assessment

Since some older workers and older worker candidates have physical limitations, physical assessment is an important tool in ensuring that proper job placement is accomplished. It is important to realize, however, that physical assessment tools should be used for all employees, not just older workers, since physical ability to perform a job is an important job dimension for all employees.

One tool used by many employers in Hawaii is the Job Physical Assessment Tool (Job PAT). The Job PAT was developed by the Tourism Training Council of the Commission on Employment and Human Resources. It was developed as a means to mainstream more physically handicapped, or "physically challenged," adults into the workplace.

The Job PAT is intended to be used with all job applicants and incumbents to ensure that the physical demands of the job can be met. First, employers are asked to complete an assessment questionnaire to determine the exact parameters of physical demands that are required. For example, the Job PAT asks, "How often is sitting (climbing, lifting, etc.) required on the job?" along with such questions as, "Are the following visual capabilities required on the job? (depth perception, color vision, etc.)" The questionnaire is completed by the employer for each job, and takes about twenty minutes a job to complete.

Next, the Job PAT examines job redesign and restructuring issues, such as the opportunities for job-sharing, part-time work, and flexible hours. Finally, this form is used to review with all job candidates the physical requirements necessary in each job. By using a systematic approach, any type of discrimination is avoided, and all job candidates, including older workers, are placed into positions for which they are suited.

For more information on the Hawaii Job PAT, contact the Tourism Training Council, Commission on Employment and Human Resources, 335 Merchant Street, Suite 354, Honolulu, Hawaii, 96813, or call (808) 548-2630.

Challenges of Career Development

Keeping older workers productive and challenged in the workplace no doubt will become one of the biggest concerns for businesses today and tomorrow. With fewer younger workers entering the work force, it makes sense to investigate ways in which businesses can more effectively manage careers of mid-life and older workers so that older employees will continue to make valuable contributions to the organization.

The AARP Worker Equity Department has published a brochure titled *How to Train Older Workers*. This publication highlights three serious problems faced by older employees: career burnout, career plateauing, and career obsolescence.[7]

Career Burnout

Burnout can best be described as emotional and /or physical exhaustion, typically caused by intense job stress. Some of AARP's suggestions for combating career burnout include:

• Job redesign or cross-training

• Special temporary assignments

• Reassignment as trainers or consultants

• Stress management training

• Sabbatical leaves

Career Plateauing

When there is little or no chance of promotion, employees may feel that they are stagnated or plateaued on the job. Some offered solutions by AARP include:

- Reassignment to temporary projects

- Investigation of alternate career paths

- Evaluation of opportunities for training and development

- Use of performance appraisals to determine problem areas as well as opportunities for improvement

Career Obsolescence

With technologies advancing at alarming rates, many employees face the reality that the current work world does not require the special skills they possess. AARP offers these solutions for dealing with career obsolescence:

- Retraining courses for employees whose skills are outdated

- Career planning workshops to permit employees to discover career options

- Educational assistance programs, and encouragement for employees to take advantage of these programs

- Involvement in professional organizations so that employees will become aware of technological changes, and will take responsibility for their continuing growth and development

One company faced with a serious case of career obsolescence found it profited immensely by offering special assistance to its older workers. It was an electronic aerospace division in a *Fortune 500* company in New York that employed older engineers, many of whom had not kept their skills updated. The company realized that without major changes, the organization would be unable to meet future production goals.

It responded by offering a voluntary retraining program to these older workers. Training classes were held on company time at no cost to the employees. Thirty-nine of the forty enrollees successfully completed the course, thus meeting the organization's need for more qualified employees.

The company enjoyed other benefits from this process. It was able to reward older employees who had been with the company a number of years, and was able to provide a positive work climate. The company found that it derived a 1:3 direct cost-to-benefit ratio when taking into consideration what would have occurred if the training had not been conducted. The organization would have been forced to lay off the older workers, then hire younger workers. With labor shortages, particularly in technology occupations, increased costs would have been incurred in terms of higher recruiting costs, unemployment costs, and initial training costs. By providing for its older workers, the company made everyone a winner.[8]

Another high-technology company has found that through job redesign, older employees whose performance has diminished over time can be assisted. Initially this company began the program as a means to meet the needs of workers with disabilities, but has expanded to meet the needs of older workers as well.

The program can be accessed by any manager whose employee's performance has slipped. The manager initially meets with the job redesign specialist to discuss performance issues. Then the employee meets with the specialist to discuss reasons for the decrease in performance. When changes in performance are caused by health reasons, a reduced work assignment is often recommended. This organization reported a 90 percent success rate in placing redesign cases in alternate positions.[9]

In another creative-thinking company, career counseling teams are available to assist both younger and older workers in determining career development needs. The team is instrumental in determining whether transfer is appropriate, timing of a transfer, and other issues. This program has been effective in providing career paths for entry-level workers seeking to move up on the career ladder.[10]

Training for older workers means addressing initial training needs for new workers, along with assessment, re-training, and development needs for older workers within the work force. A solid training and development program can be instrumental not only in meeting immediate organizational goals, but also in retaining key employees, which will help the organization meet its long-term objectives.

Supervisory Training: Managing a Diverse Work Force

Managers today face myriad new and different issues from those of yesterday. Today's supervisors must know how to recruit, train, manage, and retain all of today's workers—younger, older, male, female, minority, disabled. Today's managers must be given the tools to be effective with the diverse work force of today and tomorrow.

Managers accustomed to supervising one type of worker may find themselves ill-equipped to respond to the variety of "new" worker issues. For example, food service managers who have traditionally supervised young workers may find that their management skills are inadequate for supervising an older work force. As a response to this change, many organizations are developing management training programs that address those specific needs.

McDonald's, Kentucky Fried Chicken Corporation, and Hardee's Food Systems are three companies that have developed management sensitivity training programs to introduce their management teams to recruiting, training, managing, and retaining older workers. In each of these companies, managers have typically supervised young workers, and are not familiar with the differences in managing older workers.

Hardee's has developed an intensive one-day training program for all its managers. New Horizons focuses on providing how-to information on employing older workers, as well as identifying attitudes and perceptions about these workers. Delving into attitudes was important to Hardee's in developing the program, as the company recognized that many managers—young managers in particular—were uncomfortable in training and managing people old enough to be their parents or grandparents. Hardee's also recognized that myths are still prevalent about older workers, and felt that the training session would provide a good opportunity to discuss the myths and the realities and to swap success stories.

New Horizons contains some of the following components in its sensitivity training program:

- Discussion of the aging process

- Review of labor demographics and the need for alternate staffing sources

- Statement of Hardee's philosophy and policy on employing older workers

- Discussion of the myths regarding older workers, as well as sharing of success stories in hiring older workers

- Guidelines for more effectively recruiting older workers, including guidelines for working with government-funded employment and training programs

- Review of the Hardee's recruitment support materials that target older workers

- Guidelines for selecting and training older workers

• Case studies and discussion on management issues

• Action planning exercises for making it work

Training Support Available to Employers

A number of government-funded employment and training programs provide services to employers who wish to employ older workers. These programs generally fall into two categories: those that operate with funds from the Jobs Training Partnership Act (JTPA), and those that operate with funds through Title V of the Older Americans Act. JTPA programs are administered by local Private Industry Councils (PICs), and employers can learn what programs are available for training assistance by contacting their local PICs. Programs funded through the Older Americans Act have locations throughout the United States and are run through national offices. Title V programs are called Seniors in Community Service Employment Programs and can be reached by calling their national or local offices. A directory of national offices is in the Appendix.

Preretirement Training

Many companies have recognized that preretirement planning is not only desired by older employees, but it is good business in transitioning workers in and out of the workforce. More detailed information on preretirement planning and training is discussed in chapter 7.

Summary

Training is indeed the key for employers in maintaining a work force able to meet the needs of a rapidly changing world. By providing training that meets the needs of an aging work force, employers will be able to effectively recruit and retain new workers. By developing strategies to assist workers with career burnout, career plateauing, and career obsolescence, employers will discover they are providing cost-effective solutions that are productive and humane. Sensitivity training to assist managers in supervising a diverse work force will provide the basis for a solid program that encourages the employment of a varied work force to meet labor needs.

Notes

1. See Robert B. Revere, "High-Tech Training for the Unemployed Senior Citizens in Northern Virginia," *Older Worker News*, Third Quarter, 1988, pp. 2–3.
2. See David Ghitelman, "The Teaching Challenge: Getting Through to Grown-ups," *Meetings and Conventions*, p. 61.
3. See "How to Train Older Workers in Computers," *The Older Worker*, August 1988.
4. Interview with Pat Breathitt.
5. See Katherine J. Buckovetz, Ph.D., "Charting the Right Path for Program Enrollers Through Skillful Assessment," *Employment and Training Newsline*, May 1988, pp. 1–2.
6. Ibid.
7. See *How to Train Older Workers*, Worker Equity Department, American Association of Retired Persons, 1988, p. 5–6.
8. See *32 Million Older Americans: A Handbook for Emloyers on the Trends, Issues, Laws, and Strategies Pertaining to Older Worker Utilization*, National Urban League, Inc., pp. 21–22.
9. Ibid.
10. Ibid.

5
Dollars and Sense: Compensation Issues and the Older Worker

If a man has important work, and enough leisure and income to enable him to do it properly, he is in possession of as much happiness as is good for any of the children of Adam.
—R. H. Tawney

If businesses are to redesign the workplace to attract and retain older workers, they must include a close examination of compensation and benefits. Some complex issues that employers will need to analyze are:

- How much should older workers be paid, considering their varied lifestyles and motivations for work?

- What do employers need to know about Social Security and how it affects older workers' earnings?

- What benefits programs are important to older workers?

- How should employers work to control benefits costs when employing older workers?

- How important are eldercare benefits and wellness programs for employment of older workers?

- What pension design issues are essential for the continued employment of older workers?

- How does Social Security affect the total benefit program for senior workers?

- How should compensation programs be communicated to older workers for maximum results?

All these issues are becoming increasingly important in employment of older workers, both in attracting them and in retaining them.

Salary: How Much to Pay?

Older workers have a variety of motivations for work—financial, social, and personal. Employers have discovered that since many work for reasons other than financial, there is an opportunity to offer less money. However, under age discrimination law, it is illegal to offer older workers less money than younger workers when they perform the same functions.

Employers need to recognize that differentiated motivation for work is not sufficient rationale for paying the older adult less money, unless there is less work, restricted duties, limited work hours, or other significant differences.

Older workers should be paid for their contribution to the workplace. For many employers, this may equate to a higher wage, especially for those individuals whose work and life experiences make them even more valuable on the job. However, employers should exert caution in this area as well. In many states, it is illegal to pay someone more or less money on the basis of age alone.

One food service employer recognized that its older workers were extremely valuable employees because they demonstrated higher levels of customer service, loyalty, and safety. Because of these factors, the company wanted to attract more older workers, and thought that by paying a higher starting wage to older workers, it could do a better job of attracting them. The company recognized, however, that in many states in which it operated it was illegal to pay employees more solely on the basis of age.

The company decided to offer all employees a higher starting wage if they possessed more experience—work *and* life experience. By simply using a formula that included experience as a basis for pay, it was able to attract the older workers it wanted.

Many employers have found that by using a wage/salary range, as opposed to a fixed wage rate, variables such as experience can be included in determining starting pay. The use of ranges can be helpful in differentiating pay for performance as a means to retain valuable, contributing employees.

Pay and Social Security Benefits

Many older workers receive Social Security benefits, and may be concerned with how their earnings will affect these benefits. As of January 1, 1990, the earnings guidelines for Social Security were:

- Persons younger than sixty-five could earn up to $6,840 without jeopardizing their Social Security benefits.

- Persons sixty-five through sixty-nine could earn up to $9,360 without jeopardizing their Social Security benefits.

- Persons seventy and older could earn as much as they wished without jeopardizing their Social Security benefits.

Further, the benefit reduction for those sixty-five through sixty-nine was one dollar for three dollars; in other words, for every three dollars earned over the $9,360 amount, Social Security benefits were decreased by one dollar. For those younger than sixty-five, the benefit reduction was one dollar for two dollars; or, for every two dollars earned over the $6,840 limit, Social Security benefits were decreased by one dollar.[1]

These income guidelines change each year, so employers need to remain updated by checking with their benefit consultant each year, or call Social Security's twenty-four-hour, toll-free number for information regarding this and other questions. The number is 1-800-234-5772, and replaces thirty-four separate numbers that in the past were used for information.[2] This number should be a timesaver for employers and employees alike, who may have called many numbers before getting the right person. It may also save a trip to the local Social Security office.

Many employers are recognizing that Social Security benefits and earnings guidelines are difficult to understand, and that employees may need assistance in determining how many hours they should work, and at what rate. Kelly Services, for example, has developed a brochure for its older employees titled, *How Temporary Work Affects Your Social Security Checks*. It includes answers to such questions as:

• How much can I earn and still receive benefits?

• What counts as earnings?

• Are any of my benefits taxable?

By addressing these issues, it shows older adults who may be considering work at Kelly just what they might expect to earn, considering their income from Social Security.

Hardee's Food Systems has given its managers an information sheet that includes an earnings guidelines chart so that managers and employees can sit down together and discuss scheduling issues. Salary earnings and hours similar to the Hardee's information sheet are outlined in table 5–1.

Hardee's managers are reminded not to assume that all older adults receive Social Security benefits, or that all older adults want to manage their hours so as not to exceed Social Security earnings limitations. Many older adults who are eligible for Social Security benefits may choose to work full time, decreasing their Social Security benefits, yet increasing their take-home pay. Table 5–2 demonstrates how older workers can earn more than the income guidelines, and take home more pay, since the Social Security benefits are reduced according to the one-to-three or one-to-two ratio. Hardee's asks its managers to counsel older employees, allowing the employee to make the decision on how many hours to work.

Table 5–1
Social Security Earnings Guidelines[a]

Wage per Hour	Age		
	Under 65	65–69	70+
$ 3.35	39 hours	53 hours	Unlimited
$ 3.85	34 hours	46 hours	Unlimited
$ 4.00	32 hours	45 hours	Unlimited
$ 5.00	26 hours	36 hours	Unlimited
$ 7.50	17 hours	24 hours	Unlimited
$10.00	13 hours	18 hours	Unlimited
$15.00	8 hours	12 hours	Unlimited
$20.00	6 hours	9 hours	Unlimited

[a]The number of hours that can be worked per week without jeopardizing Social Security benefits

Table 5–2
Potential Earnings Chart

Earnings	Amount over Limit	Amount Deducted from Benefits	Net Increase Over Benefits*
Under 65:			
$10,000	$ 3,160	$1,580	$ 8,420
20,000	13,160	6,580	13,420
65–69:			
$10,000	$ 640	$ 213	$ 9,787
20,000	10,640	3,546	16,454

*Net increase may vary according to the amount the individual receives from Social Security. This calculation assumes that benefits exceed deductions.

Importance of Benefits

Just as there are older worker subsets with different lifestyles, motivations, and needs, there are varying responses to the importance of benefits in the workplace. For example, for the woman who is divorced, is not eligible for Social Security, and has never worked, the need for full-time work and full benefits is of utmost importance. However, for the employee who retired with a comfortable pension and retirement benefits, is receiving Social Security, and is eligible for Medicare, employer-provided benefits may not be as important.

Increasingly, employers are turning to cafeteria-style benefits, allowing the employee to choose the kinds of benefits needed. This versatility permits all workers, not just older workers, to receive a variety of benefits that meet their needs. For example, in using cafeteria-style benefits, a young single person can opt for little or no retirement/pension savings, a higher deductible on health insurance, and more take-home pay. An employee with a family can choose a lower deductible, family coverage, and dental insurance. An older worker may choose some combination of group health insurance, life insurance, and retirement income. The employer then pays only for those benefits used by its employees, instead of paying for benefits that may be unused by certain employee groups. Older workers particularly enjoy the ability of the benefit plan to meet their different needs.

To establish a good compensation and benefit plan, many companies are investigating the use of employee-employer task forces that include representatives from the insurance carriers. Employee representatives are selected from a variety of worker groups, covering the diversity of worker lifestyles, ages, sexes, and other dimensions. By permitting the involvement of employees, companies assure that worker needs are being adequately addressed.

Cost Containment and Wellness Programs

Many organizations fear that more older workers means more unhealthy, unproductive workers—and higher insurance costs. However, businesses can take measures to manage these benefit costs, says a report by the Washington Business Group on Health and the American Association of Retired Persons.[3] Here are some of the suggestions in this report:

- Listen to the needs and concerns of older workers who use the benefits.
- Alter benefit plans to meet the changing needs of older workers.
- Offer on-site wellness programs, screening, and education programs.[4]

Recommendations for methods to determine older workers' suggestions and ideas include attitude surveys, task forces, focus groups, employee meetings, and informal discussions. Some organizations conduct annual meetings to discuss concerns and ideas on compensation and benefits programs exclusively.

The next step is taking action. Meet with insurance representatives about changing work force needs; investigate programs these companies can offer that actually benefit the changing employee base. Consider other insurers if the current programs are not flexible enough.

Wellness programs, screening, and education are important steps many companies fail to take, especially in focusing on special requirements of older workers. And, says the report from the Washington Business Group on Health and AARP, many older workers can reap big benefits from this focus on health and productivity. In return, businesses reap tremendous benefits from worksite wellness programs, as these programs not only tend to contain health costs, but also improve employee morale, productivity, and community relations and goodwill.

Older workers must be encouraged to participate in wellness programs, as they are often the least likely to use them. Often, older workers do not participate because they feel excluded from the activities—whether or not this is reality. One way these activities tend to exclude older adults is to use only youth-oriented rock music during aerobics and exercises classes, or to offer only high-impact aerobics, instead of low-impact aerobics that are often preferred by older adults. Participation rates by all employee groups will be increased by using a variety of music, exercise options, and older and younger class instructors. Offer walking, golfing, bowling, and square dancing, as these are more appealing to older workers.

Many older adults also prefer self-directed activities that allow them to establish their own goals and the activities that lead to their goals. Program staff then periodically check in on these activities, monitoring progress.

Successful wellness programs possess certain characteristics, reports Robert Levin of the Washington Business Group on Health. These traits are:

- **Doctors' support.** The credibility of wellness programs is enhanced when older workers see the support and involvement of physicians.

- **Spouse involvement.** Results improve when the family is involved, especially in behavior modification classes for weight control, nutrition, or smoking cessation.

- **Health-risk focus.** Older adults are more likely to respond if the program's focus is not on older workers, but on a particular health risk, such as high blood pressure or heart disease.

- **Credible, enthusiastic staff.** Employees tend to become involved in wellness programs when they are staffed with energetic, knowledgeable staff. Older employees respond best to a staff trained in dealing with older adults and sensitive to aging issues. Seniors usually resent a condescending attitude.

- **Individual achievement recognition.** Since many older adults don't possess the same physical endurance, emphasize personal achievement toward individual goals.[5]

Screening and education also play an important role in improving cost containment. Classes, seminars, and workshops on health-related topics receive high ratings from older workers. Cholesterol testing, blood pressure testing, and other on-site testing measures can be an excellent way for employees to become aware of health issues, and can encourage participation in wellness program activities.

Employers can continue health education through information included in payroll stuffers, employee newsletters, information meetings, direct mailings to employees' homes, bulletin board notices, self-quizzes, and pamphlet racks. Stress the company's interest in encouraging healthy living and its commitment to wellness programs.

For additional information on the report developed by the Washington Business Group on Health, write for *Wellness Programs for Older Workers and Retirees*, (fifteen dollars each), Washington Business Group on Health, 229½ Pennsylvania Avenue, S.E., Washington, D.C., 20003.

Eldercare and Long-term Care

As the work force continues to age, more employees are caring for and supporting elderly parents, spouses, and relatives. Employers are responding by offering long-term care and eldercare benefits to their employees.

A study by The Travelers Companies showed that between one-quarter and one-third of employees older than forty are family caregivers, spending an average of twelve hours a week in caregiving activities. Some employees spend more than thirty-five hours a week in providing care to sick family members.[6] Further, according to one survey, one in five caregivers has not had a vacation for more than two years. In a 1985 study, 11 percent of mid-life and older working women had to leave their jobs to care for an older family member.[7]

Many employers recognize that employees are affected when they must care for elderly relatives. Financially and emotionally, caring for elderly parents, spouses, and family members can be tremendously draining for the employees who must provide time, attention, and resources to caregiving. The results are increased absenteeism, tardiness, sick leave, excessive telephone use, and lowered productivity and morale. Hidden costs include frequent anxiety and depression—seen in increased usage of health benefits.

Long-term care, or eldercare, is fast becoming an employee benefit being explored by many companies struggling to keep pace with the demands of an aging work force, since many employees affected by providing eldercare are older than forty. Some companies offer nursing home, home health, and adult day care for employees, spouses, and parents, and for retirees and their spouses.

However, many employers are hesitant to offer these benefits, citing high costs, low employee interest, and unfavorable tax treatment, says the International Foundation of Employee Benefit Plans. According to this report, more than two-thirds of respondents in a survey had little or no interest in sponsoring a long-term care plan, with only 4 percent having a strong interest, and about 30 percent indicating a moderate interest.

In another report, sponsored by the Washington Business Group on Health, 38 percent of the companies queried said they were investigating the possibility of offering some long-term care benefit. Further, 77 percent of the respondents in this survey indicated "some" or "strong" interest in an employee-paid benefit.[8]

This report is similar to the International Foundation of Employee Benefit Plans report in that employers perceived the barriers to offering this benefit being the high cost, few products from which to choose in the marketplace, and fear of employee and/or government pressure to provide benefits.

Employee interest is growing in the area of employer-sponsored, long-term care insurance, recent studies report. One, conducted by the University of Maryland Center on Aging, indicated that almost 70 percent of full-time working respondents older than eighteen would be interested in purchasing insurance through their employer.[9]

Many companies are responding to this increasing employee need by investigating benefit alternatives. One is

Senior Partners, a nonprofit partnership of two visiting nurses associations in Danvers, Massachusetts, which has created a program called Elder Care. It offers a variety of services for employees who are caregivers, including seminars, support groups, counseling, in-home assessments, and respite care. The services are determined by the package the employer chooses. Senior Partners offers a proposal to employers interested in offering eldercare benefits, and prices each proposal on a per-employee basis.[10]

Elder Care Solutions, a private geriatric care management practice in Louisville, Kentucky, provides information, referral, professional guidance, and in-home services to employer groups. Merrily Orsini, president of the organization, describes the services offered to corporations as being similar to many of the Employee Assistance Programs (EAPs) already offered in some companies—but it focuses on aging issues. For companies using Elder Care Solutions, employees may call a number for phone consultation, assessment, education, specific services, and followup. Orsini also offers corporate seminars on such topics as, "What Can I Expect as My Parents Grow Older?" and "Legal Issues and Interventions."[11]

Many leading employers offer long-term care benefits as a means to attract more older workers and to improve productivity, morale, and retention rates among current employee ranks. Procter & Gamble and American Express are two firms offering such insurance to their employees, which can be purchased for themselves, their spouses, and their parents. These firms do not contribute to the premiums; employees who opt for the insurance pay for it through payroll deduction. Costs to the employee are 20 percent to 30 percent less than if purchased independently.[12]

At each firm, about 10 percent of the employees have purchased the benefit, with most of those participating being older than forty. American Express has extended this insurance offer to its retirees, but very few have elected the insurance, as many already have private insurance.

Champion International, a forest products and paper manufacturer with more than thirty thousand employees, offers corporate assistance to employees who are caregivers. They have offered this benefit since 1981.

Champion's program offers benefits to employees in four major areas:

- **Counseling.** Champion offers up to three visits to a physician or a licensed psychologist for employees and elderly dependents.

- **Information.** Champion has developed a booklet, *Caring for the Elderly*, with the assistance of the National Council on the Aging. It offers information on stress management and medical and support services.

- **Financial assistance.** A Dependent Care Assistance Plan is offered as part of the flexible benefits plan. Employees can pay for the plan with pretax dollars. Under current tax law, employees may place up to five thousand dollars in tax-deferred "dependent care accounts."

- **Family care leave.** The Champion plan offers employees up to 180 days of unpaid leave for care of elderly family members. All company benefits remain in force during the leave period.[13]

Other big employers also offer a wide variety of benefits. Honeywell, Inc., for example, provides employees with counselors who can identify community resources that provide services to family members. The Travelers Companies conducts a caregiving fair that attracts more than seven hundred employees, and offers caregiving seminars that attract fifty to one hundred employees. Pepsico offers its employees in Westchester, New York, a seventy-page booklet called *Elder Care Resource Guide.* Robert Wilson, employee assistance director of Travelers, emphasizes that eldercare benefits need not be costly, and stresses that information and support are often what are needed most by employees.[14]

While the market for long-term care insurance is still in its infancy, nearly all large insurance companies are investigating this option, says a report of the Employee Benefit Research Institute, titled *Shifts in the Tide: The Impact of Changing Demographics on Employers, Employees, and Retirees.* In 1987 only about seventy-five companies offered any long-term care insurance, but the growth in this area has been tremendous.[15] Employers should be on the lookout for many varieties of new plans in the upcoming years, and should consult with their insurance carrier for updates and developments.

When investigating long-term care insurance, employers need to take several factors into consideration, says Mercer-Meidinger-Hansen's report, *Long-term Care: The Newest Employee Benefit.*

- Long-term care (LTC) plans should be coordinated with medical and government services to eliminate gaps in coverages for employees, and to ensure that the most cost-effective alternatives are being used.

- LTC plans should be coordinated with services that are currently provided in the marketplace, so that there isn't an artificial increase in the demand for long-term care services. The report gives the example of Alaska, which wanted to provide LTC coverage for its seven thousand state-employee retirees. It was discovered that there were only six hundred nursing home beds in the entire state, most of which were already being used by Medicare patients.

- Levels of coverage should be appropriate, which is difficult to determine when such new coverage of this sort is being offered.

- The plan should permit shared risk among the employer, provider, and beneficiary.[16]

All in all, the report concludes that a quick fix still does not exist in the marketplace today, and that employers will have to work with insurance carriers to develop and design LTC plans to meet the needs of employees and employers. The report also warns employers to try to "get everything right the first time," because it is difficult to make changes in LTC plans once initiated, since employees usually begin to build reserves with their first premium payments. The report concludes that long-term care and eldercare benefits are growing health-care issues that are gaining public attention and awareness, and are likely to be the hot benefit issue for the 1990s. Larger companies that can afford to negotiate specifically designed programs will be watched by both employers and insurers as these groups decide whether they should enter this new market.[17]

Pensions

As the work force continues to age, the amount of money to be received upon retirement as income becomes an increasingly important issue. While Social Security benefits are an essential ingredient, they are not intended to be the only source of retirement income. As income levels increase, the percentage of Social Security benefits as a portion of total replacement income declines. For example, replacement income for a married employee with a nonworking spouse making fifteen thousand dollars would be 63 percent derived from Social Security benefits; an employee making sixty thousand dollars with a nonworking spouse would receive only 24 percent of replacement income from Social Security.[18]

Employers assist employees in providing for replacement income to augment Social Security benefits through pension plans and savings plans. Savings plans, while a popular way to help employees fill the gap, should not be relied upon exclusively for retirement income planning, since such plans are not mandatory and do not totally restrict early withdrawals.

Pension plans vary widely, offering differing levels of benefits based upon years of service, earnings levels, and age at retirement. There are two basic types of pension plans—defined benefit plans and defined contribution plans. In defined contribution plans, the employer contributes a percentage of the employee's salary into the fund; in defined benefit plans, the amount and rules determining the benefit are set in advance, and the company must build up a reserve fund to meet its pension liabilities.

Economists recently have discovered that defined benefit pension plans may contribute to continued trends of early retirement. In a study conducted by three Harvard University economists surveying twenty-five hundred pension plans, defined benefit plans make early retirement incentives more attractive. In many, the increase in benefits beyond age sixty-two often doesn't exceed the perceived payoffs in remaining in the workplace. In one company, for example, it was discovered that while only 2 percent of employees retired at fifty-three or fifty-four, 10 percent of employees retired at fifty-five through sixty. At sixty through sixty-two, the number jumps to 17 percent, with only 10 percent left by age sixty-five.[19]

If employers are to encourage the employment of older workers, defined benefit pension plans should be reexamined to determine if they are in fact offering additional incentives for early retirement. In some cases, employers may want to change their benefit plans.

Further, pension plans should be examined to determine whether they are flexible enough to meet individual needs, reports Richard Burkhauser, economics professor at Vanderbilt University, at a congressional seminar, "Older Workers in an Aging Society." Harold Sheppard, University of South Florida's director of International Exchange Center on Gerontology, agrees, saying that while many older adults want to work part time after early retirement, many existing benefit plans do not permit this flexibility.[20]

Employers need to evaluate the goals of their benefit plans, and assess how well these plans meet the needs of an aging work force. Studies should be conducted to evaluate the results of these benefit plans, and to analyze whether current benefit structures are encouraging—intentionally or not—early retirement. Employees should be polled to determine whether these benefit plans are meeting their needs for retirement and for continued employment. Many employers are creating task forces of employees, management representatives, and insurers to determine what changes and modifications should be made to allow the flexibility needed in an aging work force.

One employer, for example, found that while its organizational goals were to employ its older workers beyond their retirement from full-time employment, it was only able to protect the employees' pension benefits by using an employee leasing company to hire its older workers. While this method met goals, the company realized it was going to a lot of extra expense and effort to work around the design of an outdated pension program. The company developed and implemented a new pension plan, with input from older employees, the insurer, and management staff.

Postretirement Medical Benefits

As the work force continues to age, more employees are concerned with the health benefits provided for them after retirement. In 1984, an estimated 3.1 million retirees between forty-five and sixty-four, and 6 million retirees sixty-five and older, had insurance from postretirement health plans.[21] And, since most employers fund these benefits on a current cost basis, employers may be realizing that some funding issues such as health-care costs continue to rise, and life expectancies increase. In fact, the Employee Benefit Research Institute has found that corporations may be liable for about $169 billion in unfunded commitments.[22]

Another difficulty facing employers is a new Financial Accounting Standards Board ruling that requires employers to report unfunded liability for postretirement health benefits in a financial statement.[23] Since this ruling will affect the value of stocks, the likely consequence will be employers' changing to an advance funding for these plans or reddesigning health benefits, perhaps even reducing benefits. However, with increasing pressure from an aging work force to provide benefits for retirement, this is likely to become an area for negotiation and debate between employer and employees. There is also some discussion that employers may fight for tax relief in this area.

Medicare

Medicare is divided into Part A, Hospital Insurance, and Part B, Supplementary Medical Insurance. Generally, Part A covers inpatient hospital care, with a deductible and co-insurance, and certain other types of care, and Part B covers 80 percent of doctor bills up to Medicare's "reasonable and customary" limits, after a deductible.[24] Most retiree medical plans are designed to supplement Medicare or fill in coverage gaps.

Many employers are confused about when Medicare is considered to be the primary carrier and when the employer group insurance plan is the primary carrier, especially for "unretired" retirees. Recent legislative changes have determined the employer's insurance plan as the primary carrier, "by reason of employment" rather than "by reason of retirement."[25]

Employers may want to explore the opportunities of offering retirees medical benefits by administering Medicare themselves. Under a new federal program—the Medicare Insured Groups (MIGs) program—employers are able to offer retirees health benefits directly. Congress has authorized $600 million a year to fund this program.

Companies that wish to offer the program will be reimbursed 95 percent of their previous expenditures for members of the group (modified by national averages). The program is voluntary—only retirees and employees who wish to opt for this program will receive benefits under the program.

The intent of the program is to eliminate duplication and cut down on the questionable use of health care, as well as to assist in reducing the amount of unfunded future health benefits for retired employees.

Many corporations are exploring the use of MIGs, with only two companies having gained final approval for implementation. Amalgamated Life Insurance Company of New York, in conjunction with Amalgamated Textile and Clothing Workers Union, and Chrysler Corporation, in conjunction with United Auto Workers Union and Blue Cross/Blue Shield of Michigan, are the two firms that offer the program to their retirees. Both hope to offer extended benefits and hold down health-care costs through the program. The benefit to firms that can save money through the program will be a 5 percent allocation from savings to defray administration costs.

Initially, the program will be closely monitored by Medicare to ensure that beneficiaries receive the benefits they deserve. On-site visits and periodic reviews will determine compliance.

While-this concept is still very new, many employers may want to explore it, studying the results from the large employers that are likely to implement the program. Certainly, for those employers that have had successes in controlling health care costs, there may be some opportunities to offer more benefits while keeping costs low.[26]

Social Security

This chapter earlier discussed the effect of earnings on Social Security benefits. The question that remains is employers' role in explaining Social Security benefits, rules, and procedures to employers.

As employees reach age fifty-five, learning more about Social Security and how wages will affect their benefits becomes increasingly important. Employers will want to be able to provide information and counseling to employees about retirement income and other benefits.

Many employers have developed educational materials for their older employees to assist in this learning process. Detailed pamphlets, brochures, payroll stuffers, and workbooks have been produced by some employers. If the employer works with a benefits consulting firm, the firm may also be able to provide the employer with information-packed booklets to answer basic questions about Social Security. For example, Mercer-Meidinger-Hansen provides its client companies with booklets titled *Guide to Social Security and Medicare*. It is a forty-page booklet that is updated annually, intended to be a take-home piece for all employees.

Some companies provide information seminars on Social Security, Medicare, and other retirement issues. More details on these educational programs will be covered in Chapter 7.

While it is increasingly important for employers to provide as much information as possible on how to apply for Social Security, who is eligible, and what benefits are available, there are two bits of information that all employers should be certain to share with employees. The first is that all employees older than sixty-five should investigate applying for Social Security benefits, even if they are still working. In many cases, they may be eligible for Social Security benefits. An individual earning less than the cap could reap full benefits. Even employees with wages above the earnings cap—since their earnings are not penalized on a dollar-for-dollar basis—may be eligible for benefits. Employees also should know earnings limitations for Social Security, as well as the penalty ratios. Even those who earn more than the cap may be eligible for benefits.

All in all, employees will appreciate the information and the time and attention given to them by their employer on Social Security benefits education. The smart employer will recognize that by spending a bit of time on this topic, employees will be more likely to remain loyal, working with the organization to meet the staffing needs of the company and their own income goals.

Summary

There are many challenges and opportunities for the employer facing an aging work force. Never before have employer compensation packages—salary, pensions, wellness programs, eldercare, long-term care, and retiree health benefits—been of so much interest to employee groups. And, as the work force continues to age, there will be increasing interest in and attention to these important issues.

Employers who see the importance of meeting these changing needs and providing compensation packages that adequately attract and reward older employees must closely evaluate the appropriateness of their various benefit programs. In many cases, especially where corporate programs unintentionally encourage early retirement, employers encouraging the productive employment of older workers beyond normal retirement years need to revamp old programs to meet new corporate employment goals.

Programs such as eldercare, long-term care, wellness programs, and retiree health benefits continue to be critically important to the growing population of older employees. Employers will want to investigate ways to add and expand coverage or at least to offer alternatives through more flexible benefit packages.

Further, employers need to continually reeducate their employees on the changing benefits arena, and need to include employees, especially older ones, in the redesign and reeducation process. Employers find that employees are more open to these changes when they are involved in the process.

Insurers, employees, and employers should meet on an ongoing basis to evaluate and implement changes in compensation that adequately reflect the changes in the work force, and the needs of this new group of employees. By responding to these needs, employers will be able to meet staffing and employment goals.

Notes

1. See Mercer-Meidinger-Hansen interoffice correspondence, October 19, 1989.
2. See "Social Security Sets Up New Services To Help Public Get More Information Easier," *The Older Worker*, November 1988, p. 3.
3. See "Groups Offer Advice in Managing Health Care Costs, Utilization of Older Workers," *The Older Worker*, September 1988, p. 7.
4. Ibid.
5. See "Wellness Programs for Older Workers Can Keep Them Healthy and on the Job" *The Older Worker*, May 1988, pp. 3–4.
6. See "Thinking About Starting an Eldercare Program?" *The Aging Workforce*, December 1987.
7. See "More Firms Aid Workers Who Care for Older Relatives." *AARP News*, September 1987.
8. See "Employers Not Interested in Offering Long-Term Care Benefits, Survey Finds" *The Older Worker*, November 1988, p. 5.
9. See "Study Shows Workers Want Employer-Sponsored Long-Term Care Insurance," *The Older Worker*, March 1989, p. 4.
10. See "Program Helps Older Workers Who Are Also Caring for a Spouse or Relative," *The Older Worker*, September 1988, p. 8.
11. Interview with Merrily Orsini.
12. See "Two Firms Add an Extra Benefit for Employees—Long-Term Care Insurance," *The Older Worker*, June 1988, p. 7.
13. Ibid.
14. See "More Firms Aid Workers Who Care for Older Relatives," *AARP News*, September 1987.
15. See "Shifts in the Tide: The Impact of Changing Demographics on Employers, Employees, and Retirees," *EBRI Issue Brief*, April 1988, p. 10.
16. See *Long-Term Care: The Newest Employee Benefit*, William M. Mercer-Meidinger-Hansen, Inc., 1988, pp. 5–6.
17. Ibid., p. 12.
18. See Mary Riebold and Gary Montesano, *The Retirement Planning Spectrum*, William M. Mercer-Meidinger-Hansen, Inc., 1988, p. 5.
19. See "Defined Benefit Pensions May Contribute to Early Retirement Trend, Economist Says," *The Older Worker*, January 1989.
20. See "Panel Calls for More Flexible Pensions," *The Older Worker*, May 1988, p. 5.

21. See "Shifts in the Tide: The Impact of Changing Demographics on Employers, Employees, and Retirees," *EBRI Issue Brief*, April 1988, p. 8.
22. See "Future of Retiree Health Benefits Uncertain, Study Says," *The Older Worker*, November 1988, p. 8.
23. Ibid.
24. See *Retiree Health Benefits: Plan Designs for a Changing World*, William M. Mercer-Meidinger-Hansen, Inc., 1989, p. 2.
25. See "HCFA Regs Affect Rehired Retirees." *The Older Worker*, July 1988, p. 8.
26. See "Privatizing Medicare? New Program Hands Its Administration to Private Employers," *The Older Worker*, June 1988, p. 5.

6

Valuing Experience: Managing and Retaining an Aging Work Force

Life is a series of experiences, each one of which makes us bigger, even though sometimes it is hard to realize this.
—Henry Ford

O lder workers, by virtue of their life and work experiences, are skilled, knowledgeable, wise employees. Smart businesses recognize that there is a wealth of experience and knowledge with older workers that, when managed properly, can be a valuable asset for corporations.

What are the key issues in managing and retaining older workers? What steps must managers take in gaining full benefit of these workers? How must managers respond to the aging work force, and what changes must be made in effectively utilizing this resource? There are many questions to be answered in the management and retention of older workers. Key issues that will be discussed in detail in this chapter include:

- What are the barriers to managing and retaining older workers?

- What are the differences in work ethics and value systems of older workers, and how should managers respond to these differences?

- What do older workers want in terms of flexible work schedules and arrangements, and how can employers effectively implement these arrangements?

- How and when should job redesign be considered in dealing with the aging work force?

- What are the issues in career development, planning, and management?

- What role do performance appraisals play in the management of older workers' productivity?

- What is ageism, and how can employers avoid age discrimination in the workplace?

- What are the principles in retaining older workers, and what should businesses do in encouraging more older workers to remain with the organization?

Certainly, in creating an environment that is conducive to older workers, employers will find that more older workers are remaining on the job as productive, satisfied employees, meeting corporate goals and objectives.

Barriers in Managing and Retaining
Older Workers

While many companies are convinced of the value in attracting and retaining older workers, some barriers still exist in managing and retaining these employees in the work force, including: stereotypical thinking about older workers and, in some cases, open age discrimination, lack of flexibility in work arrangements, and misunderstandings about work ethics and value systems.

Stereotypical Thinking about Older Workers

As outlined in chapter 2, a number of myths and misperceptions persist about older workers. While many organizations may be fully committed to employing them, some managers and supervisors may have doubts about their performance capabilities. Some managers may have had a bad experience in working with older adults, and generalize this experience. Some managers may project their own concerns about a sick and frail elderly relative, and may not want to deal with older adults in the workplace, even though the health factors may be completely different.

Some managers bring to the workplace a mindset about what to expect from workers as they grow older. These supervisors may think that since older workers will be retiring soon, they can relax disciplinary guidance. It may even become accepted practice that the older workers are not expected to perform up to the same standards as their younger counterparts. This mindset creates a self-fulfilling prophecy; when less is expected, less is received. Specific strategies for managing performance and avoiding this trap will be discussed later in this chapter, as well as ways to avoid age discrimination and ageist employment actions.

Inflexibility in Dealing with Older Workers

Most older workers say a major barrier to remaining in the workplace beyond "normal" retirement age is inflexibility in work schedules and arrangements. Most older workers are presented with an all-or-nothing arrangement: either continue to work full time or retire. Many older workers agree that if more flexibility were offered in the workplace, they could remain as productive contributors.

Many older workers want flexible schedules in order to work fewer hours. Reduced work time means free hours to do the things they want to do. A less grueling timetable permits them to remain productive and energized on the job, contributing at a level that is personally satisfying and rewarding.

Flexible schedules also permit a phasing out of full-time work that leads gradually to retirement. Many older adults are frustrated because they have not had an opportunity to plan for their retirement years. A phasing process helps the organization and the individual plan for changing needs.

Until flexibility is an employment feature offered by employers, many older adults will choose to leave the work force. Flexible work alternatives and ways to implement these strategies will be discussed in this chapter.

Misunderstandings of Work Ethics and Value Systems

Many older workers, by virtue of the time in which they were born, have a different set of work ethics and values than their younger counterparts. These differences are often misunderstood by younger managers who try to supervise these workers with the same set of guidelines they would use with younger workers. The results are often misunderstandings, miscommunications, and mixed signals. Younger managers become frustrated with older workers because they do not understand this different point of reference. By learning the differences in workers of various age groups, supervisors can more effectively retain older workers and younger workers.

Values and Work Ethics

Management consultant Morris Massey, in his book *The People Puzzle* and in his presentation "What You Are Is Where You Were When . . . ," describes the ways in which individuals form their values. He concludes that the values and ethics that people develop are largely attributable to the time in which they grew up. Therefore, he says, older workers, whom he describes as "traditionalists," are much different from their younger counterparts, "challengers," because of the events that occurred in their formative years. Each, he reports, has a different and distinctive set of values and feelings toward work.[1]

Massey's theory says older workers have a much different view of authority in the workplace than younger workers. Young workers today often display little regard or respect for authority; they openly criticize and show contempt for authority figures. Older workers, in sharp comparison, value authority. They respect the boss and want to follow leadership.

Work itself takes on a different definition for younger workers than for older workers. Younger workers view work as a means to an end, with that end typically being "fun." Younger workers also expect the workplace to be enjoyable and exciting, offering challenges and opportunities. Older workers are more likely to see work as a responsibility and a duty, something expected of everyone. Older workers are more likely to live to work; younger workers are more likely to work to live.

Even promotions are viewed differently by these two worker groups. Younger workers are likely to want immediate gratification, feeling that promotions should be granted as quickly as possible. If the younger worker can learn the new job in three weeks, then that worker often feels that a promotion should be granted just that quickly. Older workers, on the other hand, are more likely to consider promotions to be earned over time. Seniority is more likely to be viewed as what one must have to move ahead.

Traditionalists and challengers often have different views on tact and honesty. Younger workers, as members of the "tell it like it is" generation, value honesty. Older workers are more likely to value tact, diplomacy, courtesy, and good manners. Reports about older workers as excellent customer service models are often made because of this ingrained value system.

Older workers are also more likely to define fairness as treating everyone the same. Consistency is the road to fairness, in these traditionalists' views. Fairness to the challenger, however, often requires a situational approach, considering the circumstances of each decision.

Traditionalists see themselves as being a part of the team—and the team comes first before self. The term "company man" reflects this value of placing the team, or the company, before self. Challengers, however, are definitely a part of the "me" generation, where self comes first. Loyalty is important only as long as personal goals are being met satisfactorily.

A synopsis of these differing views can be seen in table 6–1.

What do these differing values and work ethics mean to today's managers? They mean today's managers and supervisors must learn what divergent value systems exist for these various worker groups, and then must understand how management styles might be modified to effectively manage a diverse work force.

Table 6–1
Differences in Values for "Traditionalists" and "Challengers"

Work Issue	Younger Worker "Challenger"	Older Worker "Traditionalist"
Authority	Challenges	Respects
Meaning of work	Fun	Duty
Promotions	Automatic	Earned
Interaction	Honest	Tactful
Fairness	Situational	Consistent
Priority	Self	Team

For example, consider the manager who has always used a participative style in managing younger workers. Typically, younger workers respond positively to a management direction that allows them to be involved in the decision-making process. If an older worker enters the picture, how does that worker view this management mode? In one company, a younger manager using a participative style found that when an older worker entered the work group, a different process had to be adapted. The older worker responded negatively to the participative style, interpreting it to mean that the younger manager was abdicating authority. The older worker's behavior was then one of challenging authority, trying to show the young manager the "right" way, which was counter to company procedures.

This young manager solved the problem by talking with the older worker, and explaining that the young manager was the boss. He told the older worker, in a tactful, diplomatic way, that when he demonstrated how something was to be done, it was to be done in that way. In other words, he reinforced the older worker's value of authority, yet did it in a manner that would not challenge value systems.

Likewise, older managers who are accustomed to managing in an authoritative style that may have been effective with other older workers, may suddenly find that this management style is ineffective with younger subordinates. Management styles must be adapted to coincide with the values and work ethics of the employees.

Today, managers, young and old alike, need some assistance and guidance in developing management styles and philosophies that are more consistent with the new diversity of workers. Many manager sensitivity training programs being developed by employers are incorporating some discussion of these differing values, as well as suggestions for modification of management styles. Without training, it is unlikely that supervisors, especially new ones, are sophisticated enough to modify their management styles adequately to be as responsive in a diverse workplace as is necessary. Refer to chapter 4 for a review of management training.

Flexible Work Schedules

Many older workers find that the flexibility of alternative work schedules offers them the opportunity to work and still do other things that are important to them. For example, many find that a flexible work alternative allows them to:

- maintain their stamina and health requirements
- travel with spouse, family, and friends
- work in a professional capacity on a contractual basis
- meet personal and family needs
- share a job with another professional so as to gain the personal and professional satisfaction of training a younger worker, while working only the hours necessary to meet financial obligations

Employers are discovering that when flexible work arrangements are initiated to meet the needs of this worker segment, other worker groups also benefit. Consider the flexible work needs of adult students returning to school, back-to-work mothers, dual-career couples, and single working parents—all need to balance work, home, and educational pursuits.

This section examines the varying alternate work arrangements being offered by companies, and demonstrates how flexible arrangements can promote the continued employment of older workers. Guidelines will be reviewed on how to implement effective alternative schedules.

Flex-scheduling. Flex-scheduling, often called flextime, is a work arrangement gaining in popularity among businesses because of the benefits to employees and companies alike. By implementing flextime, many companies find that productivity increases, because absenteeism and tardiness decrease. Generally, employee morale increases, because employees are more able to meet their personal commitments while juggling their work schedules.

Flextime is an arrangement in which all employees are required to work a core time period, then can come in earlier, work later, or choose the regular work schedule, such that an eight-hour day is worked. For example, with a core time period of 10:00 A.M. to 2:00 P.M., employees may come to work as early as 6:00 A.M. and leave as early as 3:00 P.M. (with a one-hour lunch), or come as late as 10:00 A.M. and leave at 7:00 P.M.

Many older workers benefit from flextime because of obligations outside of the workplace. For example, some older workers may need to care for an elderly parent or a spouse; others may have obligations to care for grandchildren. These workers can adjust their hours to fit in with errands and schedules of these others in their lives.

Employers wishing to add flextime as a benefit to their employees may also find these benefits for themselves:

- Increased productivity, because employees are able to devote their work time to work duties, not to worrying about how personal needs will be met;

- Decreased absenteeism and tardiness, because workers are able to schedule doctors' appointments, make childcare arrangements and eldercare arrangements, and do other personal chores outside of their normal work hours;

- Decreased tardiness, because many workers are able to avoid commuting problems;

- Increased morale, because employees feel they have more control over their time and their lives.

When considering flextime, employers should analyze its effect on the work force, and consider the desires of employee groups. Some specific guidelines for implementation are:

- Gain input from employees and supervisors before starting flextime. Ask employees and supervisors to outline suggestions for implementing the program, as well as ideas for ways to ensure the program's success.

- Hold a training session to communicate the new program to all employees. Start first with department managers and supervisors, understanding their concerns for operational issues in the program. Let employees know about their rights and obligations in making the program a success.

- When there are large groups of employees involved, ask workers to sign an agreement or "contract" that clearly states the hours they will work. This eliminates later misunderstandings.

- Analyze the results of the program, in terms of productivity factors, morale, tardiness, absenteeism, and profitability. Track results over a period of time.

- Give feedback to all involved employees, including ways the program is successful, and ways it could be more effective.

By using these guidelines, companies will find that a new program such as flextime can be a successful and beneficial program for the organization and employees alike.

Another type of flex-scheduling gaining popularity is the use of flex-week, flex-month, and flex-year. In these arrangements, employees have the option, within certain guidelines, to elect to work a certain number of hours within the week, the month, or the year.

Flex-week, -month, and -year are being used particularly when the employer has certain tasks to be completed within a certain time period, yet it does not matter, beyond that deadline, when the work is accomplished. For example, banks with processing departments for monthly billings are finding that a flex-month is possible to offer to employees, as long as monthly deadlines are met. This is especially appealing to many older workers who would rather have the added flexibility of choosing work hours not just within the context of the work day, but of the work month or year. This kind of flexible scheduling would permit older employees to work a certain number of hours and still have time to travel with friends, to spend with grandchildren, or to schedule elective surgery.

Control Data Corporation (CDC), a manufacturer of computers, is one company that is using older workers to meet its staffing needs. Retired employees who are interested in working are able to opt for flextime, selecting their own work schedule. Here, the core period is from 10:00 A.M. to 2:00 P.M.[2]

Obviously, older workers can benefit greatly from added flexibility in work scheduling, as do all workers. Workers wanting to further their education can schedule time to attend night or day classes; single parents can better juggle child-care responsibilities; dual-career couples can now get to the dry cleaners, stop by the drug store, and accomplish all those tasks that may be difficult with a traditional work schedule.

Part time. Many older workers have specifically indicated that part-time work arrangements would permit them the flexibility they want and need.

Part-time is appealing because older employees can still

work the job they have always worked, but at a reduced schedule that suits their physical stamina and health, or that allows them to do other things with their time.

Companies are finding that a larger staff of part-time workers can be extremely beneficial. Some of the benefits include:

- Ability to meet peak demand staffing periods

- Ability to provide on-call employees to meet temporary staffing needs

- Ability to staff special projects and tasks

- Ability to hire just enough staff to handle tasks and assignments. For example, if a new job requires twenty hours a week, a part-time worker could meet those needs less expensively than another full-time staff member.

Employers facing staffing shortages may find that by dividing one full-time job into two part-time positions, difficult positions can be filled more easily. Employers are finding that their own problems diminish when they can offer a variety of hours and work arrangements.

Companies may also find that offering part-time work may be a way to keep some workers who otherwise would consider retirement. Part-time work may help keep employees who otherwise would leave the company to start a family, return to school, or explore another career path. Part-time work is an incentive to keep key employees when they consider other options.

One of the most highly regarded part-time employment programs for older Americans is one initiated by The Travelers Companies, called the "Older Americans Program." The company has a retiree job bank of older workers who want to work on a part-time, temporary basis, filling tem-

porary jobs within the corporate headquarters in Connecticut. By using this pool of retired workers, Travelers reduces
the costs of using an outside temporary service, while utilizing the talent and experience of its retired workers.

Texas Refinery Corporation hires older workers as independent contractors for its sales force, and most work part
time to supplement Social Security. Recently, eighteen of
the top forty performers were sixty or older.[3]

Job-sharing. Job-sharing is similar to part-time work, in
that each of the job-sharers works part-time hours. However, the significant difference in job-sharing is that the two
part-time workers split a job, each performing a portion of
that job and acting as a team to complete the requirements
of the job.

The concept of job-sharing initially began with professional and technical positions; however, almost any job can
be shared. Like part-time employment, employers are seeing
that by offering job-sharing to its employees, the organization is better able to keep workers that might otherwise
leave, to recruit workers it might otherwise never recruit,
and to improve productivity and morale in the meantime.

Job-sharing is particularly appealing to companies and
employees in that it is a more structured way in which to
view flexible schedules. Since most companies have full-
time jobs, it is easy to start with that full-time job and then
divide it into two equal sections. Employees like the concept because it is easy to understand, and highly account-
able. Many employees like the concept of being part of a
team while working part-time; organizations like this concept as well, as it makes each person responsible for the
accomplishment of a set number of tasks.

Older workers find that job-sharing is a particularly
appealing alternative. Not only does it permit part-time
hours, but it also allows for a team relationship, in

which the older worker can serve as mentor or role model, giving that worker a sense of self-esteem. By being part of a team, the older worker can be in touch with what is going on within the corporation, while still working at the desired hours. Job-sharing also permits contributions at a high level of performance and competence; it is most often used with managerial, technical, and professional positions. Therefore, the older worker is permitted to make a contribution at a high level, again enhancing his or her self-esteem.

Employers benefit because job-sharing uses the older worker at a level on a par with past contributions, and they benefit from the worker's knowledge and experience. An older worker can be paired with a younger, less experienced worker, who can benefit from the team process.

Here are some job-sharing guidelines for employers:

- Carefully study positions being considered for job-sharing to ensure that they can be easily divided into two equal jobs.

- Job-sharing works best when the employees either have worked with each other or are compatible in terms of strengths, weaknesses, personality traits, etc. Work with the job-sharers to ensure compatibility.

- Devise a communications system for relaying information from one worker to the other. Some job-sharers have found that an overlap period when both are present is helpful in terms of relaying information, changes in assignments, new projects, tasks, priorities, and the like.

- Follow up with job-sharers on a regular basis, more frequently when the program is being started. Provide performance feedback on an individual as well as a team basis.

Job-sharing with older workers can be an excellent way to have other employees benefit from the experience and judgment of these workers. Job-sharing can be a great method to provide a win–win situation.

Temporary employees. Many companies are discovering that the use of temporary employees—those hired for less-than-permanent, full-time work—is an excellent method to meet staffing needs. Using temporary employees has these advantages to the organization:

- Temporary employees can assist the organization in meeting peak staffing needs, only during the times that services are needed.

- Special projects and assignments can be accomplished without long-term commitments to full-time employees.

- Employers can add temporary employees for a surge in business without worrying about having to lay off employees at a later time, and paying unemployment insurance.

- Organizations can add employees only for the period of time absolutely needed.

Many individuals, especially older workers, like the options in working on a temporary basis. Some benefits include:

- Flexibility in working only the times, days, and months desired;

- Flexibility in working only those assignments that are appealing or that meet professional and personal needs;

- Being able to "try out" new jobs and tasks, exploring new careers and directions.

Temporary workers can work directly as employees of
the company, or as employees of a temporary help agency.
Temporary help agencies are really not "agencies" at all,
but rather, employers that hire temporary workers, and
charge clients a fee for the service of their employees. When
using temporary help agencies, companies can benefit in
these ways:

- Companies can use the services for only the period of
  time needed. The company can terminate the services of
  the agency immediately upon completion of the assignment.

- Companies get guaranteed services. When a temporary
  agency worker does not meet performance standards,
  the agency usually provides a replacement worker at no
  cost to the company, if notified promptly.

- Companies have a resource to find qualified workers
  who are willing to work temporarily. Companies in
  tight labor markets may find that temporary help agencies are invaluable in finding top employees.

- Companies can request experienced, older workers to
  meet staffing needs. Many agencies are now making
  extra efforts in attracting older workers; other agencies
  are exclusively employing older workers.

Follow the guidelines listed here for maximum effectiveness in working with temporary help agencies:

- Clearly communicate with temporary help agencies the
  specific requirements for the job, including special skills
  and abilities. The more clear and concise the initial instructions, the more likely the temporary employee will
  meet expectations.

- Be prepared to acclimate temporary employees when they report to work. Provide detailed instructions and guidelines for performing the job, including performance expectations.

- Give feedback to the temporary employee. Let the employee know if performance is meeting expectations. Also, be sure to notify the agency if the temporary employee does not meet expectations.

One temporary help agency that is making efforts to attract more older workers is Kelly Services Inc. The company has initiated a special recruitment effort aimed at the older worker. It uses clubs, churches, and adult education programs to find the older employees it wants. Kelly employs older workers because it has found that older workers often prefer the flexibility of part-time and short-term assignments. In its technical division, for example, many retirees return as temporary workers for the firms from which they retired.[4]

A temporary help agency in Louisville, Kentucky has begun to provide older people as temporary workers. The agency, Senior Power, is open to workers ages fifty-plus. Employers like the service because they know that the workers sent by Senior Power are experienced, qualified workers who have enough business know-how and professional savvy to handle the complexities of a temporary assignment. Experienced workers come to Senior Power because they know they will be assigned to employers who know the value of workers with experience. Senior Power has already enlisted a number of workers with a wide range of experience—clerical workers, sales people, doctors, attorneys, managers, and technicians. It seems that many older individuals are in search of a work opportunity that permits them to work within their chosen profession on a part-time or temporary basis.

Consultants and contractual workers. Organizations are realizing that hiring full-time employees may not be the answer, given the availability of qualified, experienced consultants and contractual workers. By using consultants, companies benefit in many of the same ways as using temporary employees, with these added benefits:

- Companies buy the experience and expertise needed, for the time period needed. For special projects, a consultant may be the most economical method.

- Companies avoid paying benefits, as consultants are self-employed.

- Companies know in advance what they will pay for any given service, and are able to project the feasibility of this option.

Many older workers would like to work as consultants and contractual workers, but are unsure of how to proceed. It often takes the initiative of the employer to propose such an arrangement.

Take the example of one older worker who had retired to enjoy some leisure time pursuing hobbies and seeing more of his grandchildren. His company was desperately seeking qualified, experienced workers in a particular technical field. By inviting this retiree back as a consultant, the company was able to fill a very narrow position, and did not have to pay benefits or other taxes. The retiree was delighted to return to a place where his experience was so obviously valued, and for a job that was limited in duration. The contract for his services was designed so he could work out of his home for much of the project, during the hours and days that met his schedule for golf, hobbies, and grandchildren.

John Erdlen, president of Northeast Human Resources

Association, says older people should be considered as temporary consultants. He says many seniors are not looking for the top-paying, prestigious jobs—just an opportunity to be an individual contributor.[5]

Employee leasing. A new phenomenon in employment and staffing alternatives is sweeping the country—employee leasing. In this arrangement, an employer fires all its employees, who are then rehired by an employee leasing company. The leasing company then "rents" these employees back to the original employer, charging back wages and a service fee to handle administrative costs.

Employee leasing may be an alternative for organizations that are interested in rehiring retirees, but that are unable to do so because the cost of pension benefits or other barriers. In many cases pension benefits are ironclad because of union contracts or other circumstances that make the discontinuation of such benefits impossible or unattractive. In these cases, employers may be able to use their retired workers most effectively through a leasing company.

Leasing companies are responsible for handling all administrative duties, including payroll taxes and some management duties, such as hiring and processing of new employees. Many leasing companies provide as many services as their client company is willing to pay for.

Employers considering employee leasing, either for all employees or for certain groups, such as older workers, should follow these guidelines:

- Check references thoroughly. Call other employers that have used the services. See if the company is a member of the National Staff Leasing Association.

- Reach an understanding in advance about what services

are to be provided by the leasing company, and for what fee.

- Resolve in advance how the leasing company will handle problem employees. Work with an attorney to resolve which party will have legal responsibility for claims of discrimination and other legal matters.

While there can be many benefits in using an employee leasing company, particularly for older workers, employers that are new to this arena should carefully research the options available, making sure that leasing will be most beneficial for employees and the organization.

Telecommuting and work-at-home arrangements. Today, as many as 14 million people work at home more than eight hours a week.[6] The numbers are growing, as cities become more congested with rush-hour commuters and as individuals search for more ways to balance home and work obligations. Businesses are seeing telecommuting and other work-at-home options as a means to increase productivity and morale, decrease absenteeism and tardiness, and improve the quality and quantity of job candidates that can be attracted to the workplace, which is increasingly at home.

Many older workers would like a work-at-home arrangement, because it allows them to work in the comfort of their own surroundings, during the hours that make the most sense because of their own obligations, health, and personal productivity issues. It also eliminates the problem of transportation to and from the workplace.

Organizations find that work-at-home arrangements mean reduction of work space at the work site, decrease in turnover, and enhanced productivity and employee morale. Further, companies recognize that with telecommuting, many workers can be employed who otherwise might not have been able to come to the work site, such as a physically disabled person who is unable to drive.

One company offering a telecommuting option for its older workers is Control Data Corporation. CDC offers "flexiplace" as an option to individuals who work at home on computer terminals. The terminals are provided by the company.[7]

Phased retirement. Phased retirement is an option being offered by companies in permitting soon-to-be retired employees the opportunity to "try out" retirement. More on this option will be discussed in chapter 7.

Summary of Flexible Options

Many flexible staffing alternatives are available to provide the kind of work environment that encourages continued employment of older workers. They want and need these options, and many will remain within the work force if these alternatives are offered.

In general, employers should encourage the use of flexible work arrangements, as it helps attract and retain not only older workers, but also many "new" worker groups that need employment flexibility. Students, women, dual-career couples, single parents, disabled persons, moonlighters, career changers, and others find that flexibility is one of the factors determining their ability to remain with their current employer.

For the most effective flexible work arrangements, employers should review the following guidelines:

- Consider the employee groups, such as older workers, that are desired for recruitment and retention efforts, and then investigate the flexible options that most closely meet their needs.

- Research options used by other employers to learn from

their experience and to understand the competitive positioning in the marketplace.

- Analyze the relative cost-effectiveness of various flexible scheduling options. Some can be implemented with virtually no costs to the company; others, such as telecommuting, require careful implementation with high start-up costs.

- Continue to involve employees in such programs to determine their needs and concerns. Form an employee task force to discuss new staffing options.

Flexible staffing alternatives will continue to be one of the most sought-after employee benefits for the 1990s. Progressive employers will begin to implement these options to meet the needs of the changing work force.

Job Redesign

Many older workers could remain in the work force if jobs could be reexamined, redesigned, and restructured to meet their changing needs. What is involved in job redesign? How should jobs be redesigned to meet the needs of older workers? These are issues many companies are exploring to provide a workplace that is conducive to the effective employment of older workers.

As employers explore job redesign, some questions should be asked:

- What barriers prevent older workers from performing the job and remaining in the job as effective contributors?

- Which older workers are effective, and which are ineffective? What factors inherent in the job contribute to this difference?

- Who are the older workers who have left the job? Why did they leave, and what, if anything, could have been done to keep them?

Once these questions have been answered, it is time to reexamine the job to determine what redesign issues, if any, are appropriate as solutions to the problems. Some aspects include:

- What are the physical requirements of the job? For example, what bending, lifting, standing, and other stamina measures are important in performing the job effectively?

- What are the scheduling requirements of the job? For example, must there be a nine-to-five day, or is it possible to complete the work at other hours? Is it possible to split the work into two part-time positions, or a job-sharing arrangement?

- Must the worker be physically present to perform essential tasks? Or can the work be performed at home in a telecommuting arrangement?

- What stressful elements can be eliminated from the work environment?

- Can duties be reassigned from one position to another without disrupting the flow of work? Is it more logical for some work duties to go with other jobs?

- Can duties be restructured for more interesting, challenging, and satisfying work? For example, can duties be regrouped for more task interrelationships and a corresponding feeling of seeing the results of each task?

While many larger corporations have staff compensation specialists who are knowledgeable in job redesign, many smaller companies may have questions about how to accomplish a job redesign. Some options include:

- Consider hiring an outside compensation or management consultant to assist in the redesign process.

- Ask for assistance from a government-funded employment and training program that works closely with older workers and older worker issues.

- Consult with older workers and other employees about ways to restructure jobs for increased satisfaction and productivity.

Often, just asking employees and gaining their input is an effective and low-cost method to better understanding how jobs must change to meet the needs of a changing work force. Task forces may even be created to study the issues and identify mutually beneficial solutions.

Career Management and Development

In the past, there has been a linear approach to education, training, and career management and development. Young people went to school to gain a basic education; they went to college or vocational schools for advanced education and training, and then went on to a job. In the job, some education and training were needed to advance the individual on to higher steps in the career ladder, and to keep the employee up-to-date on technology changes. The individual continued to grow on the job until age sixty-five, when the individual retired to enjoy leisure time.

Today, however, the model is changing to meet a new

environment of increased longevity and health, advancing technology, and changing employer and employee needs. Now, students attend school, but may return again and again throughout their employment history for retraining, new skills, or second, third, or fourth career paths. Leisure may be taken in the form of sabbaticals—respites from the world of work to pursue training, travel, or self-study.

In his book *Worklife Visions*, Jeffrey Hallett discusses how career paths have drastically changed. A career path may be initially constructed, but, because of technology changes, or even because of major changes to the industry as a whole, these career paths may no longer exist. Therefore, the approach to career management becomes quite different.

Career planning and development in the workplace needs to change to keep pace with the work force. Companies cannot just look at career planning for young workers; companies must look at ways to continue planning for workers of all ages.

Workplace expectations. Workplace expectations should be focused on continued growth and evolution throughout every employee's career. Career counseling and guidance should be structured to examine where employees have been, where they are going, and what the organization is experiencing in terms of career expectations.

In the past, the expectation was for the older worker to plan for retirement, and to discontinue work. Therefore, there existed very little career coaching at that stage. In fact, if there was an expectation, it was for performance and contribution to decrease.

This model may have contributed, and may still contribute, to low performance ratings for many older workers. If the company expects little, the employee is likely to respond with a corresponding substandard performance. The power of expectations is in play, with older workers living up to the expectations of others. In fact, many older workers have reported that as they grow older, the organization may increasingly continue to give "adequate" performance ratings, even though performance has dropped. This is one of the reasons supervisors have misgivings about increased employment of older workers. Because poor performance has been acceptable in the past for older workers, some supervisors are concerned about meeting their own performance goals under these double standards.

This scenario then becomes a vicious circle, with management having low expectations of older workers and older workers living up to those low expectations, thus perpetuating the stereotype. In a 1976 study by Rosen and Jerdee, business people were asked to comment on a hypothetical "typical" thirty-year-old worker and a "typical" sixty-year-old worker. The sixty-year-older worker was rated much lower in terms of development potential and ability to perform.[8]

Management must break the cycle, and must have equally high expectations of all worker groups. Performance standards should be set and followed, and career development should be managed throughout each employee's career, not just in the early years. Only by continuing to manage expectations will outcomes begin to change.

Businesses speak out on career management. A recent survey by the American Society for Personnel Administration (ASPA—now the Society for Human Resources Management) and Commerce Clearing House (CCH) found that businesses could take steps to improve the career management of older workers. Some of those findings are:

• Specific programs need to be developed to assist senior employees with career issues, including development of new roles for older workers, and changing policies and programs in the organizational climate to facilitate employment of older employees.

- Performance management needs to be addressed with managers responsible for senior employees.

- Good senior employees need to be continually motivated to remain as contributing work force members, discouraging early retirement.[9]

In effect, the survey summarized that businesses did not have policies, procedures, and management systems in place that would adequately manage the increasing number of older workers within the workplace. Businesses recognized that changes were needed, but few had implemented policies and procedures which would encourage the continued effective employment of senior employees.

Performance appraisal. Since managing performance is a key ingredient in creating a positive work environment for older workers, supervisors need additional training in dealing effectively with performance management systems, including the performance appraisal. Often, as cited earlier, supervisors have given satisfactory performance ratings, even when the older worker's performance has been below satisfactory, because retirement is expected in the near future.

Because older workers are continuing to work beyond "normal" retirement, supervisors must give accurate, objective performance ratings. A checklist for managers of older workers might include the following:

- Is this performance appraisal a fair, objective, and accurate summation of the worker's performance for this time period?

- Have I been consistent in rating older workers and younger workers? Are my expectations the same?

- Have I been clear in my future expectations for performance? Have I clearly stated the behaviors that I expect from all employees?

- Have I had the same expectations for continued training, retraining, and development of older workers as I have for younger workers? Have I followed through in scheduling ongoing training and development activities?

- Am I providing the same kinds of career planning guidance and direction to older workers that I give to younger workers?

By using this checklist, managers can assess their commitment to the older worker, and can ensure that the same consistent and fair treatment in managing performance and long-term career development are in the best interests of the company and the older employee.

Motivating the problem older employee. One of the biggest challenges in corporations today is motivating the older employee who is bored, burned out, or otherwise unmotivated. In the past, because of the escape valve of traditional retirement age, these employees, if close enough to retirement age, would be taken care of by the system; managers did not need to take any disciplinary action.

However, in today's environment, with no customary retirement age, and no mandatory retirement except for certain select occupations, this easy way out for managers of poor older performers has been eliminated. Managers today must look to other methods to motivate and otherwise deal with the marginal older worker.

The American Association for Retired Persons offers several suggestions for motivating older workers in its resource guide, *How To Manage Older Workers*. The guide includes several motivational principles.

Principle One: Identify the needs of older workers. To motivate workers, managers must first start by understanding their needs. For older employees, these often include financial security, social interaction, and making a contribution to others.

Principle Two: Link needs to behavior. By showing the older worker that job performance is directly related to a satisfaction of a need, the manager is more likely to influence behavior.

Principle Three: Set goals for the older employee. Counsel with the older employee to set measurable, realistic, and attainable goals. Specify how performance will be measured, and what performance level is acceptable. Work with the employee in setting time frames for completion and in prioritizing goals.

Principle Four: Ensure that older employees have the means to achieve goals. If additional training or retraining is needed by the older worker, follow through to ensure that this training is made available.

Principle Five: Reward performance. When employees meet their goals, provide recognition and rewards that are appropriate given the level of achievement. Also, review the needs of older individuals, and ensure that these needs are being matched with rewards that help meet them.

Principle Six: Change the nature of work. Work becomes boring, dull, and repetitive when there are no changes over time. Provide the older employee with a change of pace, additional autonomy, or new responsibilities.[10]

By using these principles, managers can motivate their marginal older workers into acceptable performance outputs.

Age Discrimination and Ageism

What is ageism? Ageism is like racism and sexism in that it is a way of stereotyping a group of people. Where racism stereotypes people according to their race, and sexism stereotypes people according to their sex, ageism prejudges people according to their age. Ageism is much more subtle than gerontophobia, an unreasonable fear or hatred toward older people.

Ageism is the antithesis of good business, because it fails to look at people as individual contributors. It assumes facts that are not true. Ageism is a subtle, negative theme that discourages older adults from remaining in the work force, because it undermines their self-confidence and self-esteem.

Ageism and age discrimination are similar, but not the same. Ageism may not necessarily be unlawful; age discrimination is. Older workers who have been discriminated against in the workplace because of their age can fight back; ageism in the workplace often just discourages older workers from remaining in the workplace. Both age discrimination and ageism need to be eliminated from the workplace if businesses are interested in more fully utilizing the talents and abilities of America's older adults.

Age Discrimination

Employees older than forty are protected under the Age Discrimination in Employment Act (ADEA) of 1967 as amended in 1986. The act covers private employers of twenty or more workers and all federal employees. Local ordinances and state legislation cover workers older than forty in smaller companies.

The purpose of the ADEA is "to promote employment of older workers based on their ability rather than age; to prohibit arbitrary age discrimination in employment; and to help employers and workers find ways of meeting problems arising from the impact of age on employment." The ADEA's purpose, then, is not to protect older workers only from unjust hiring and firing practices, but in all terms and conditions of employment. Further, it protects those who may file a charge of discrimination under the Act.

Therefore, ADEA protects individuals in hiring, firing, promotions, training, salary, benefits, and all other aspects of the employment process. One exception is for those employers that have a bona fide occupational qualification (BFOQ) for age; in other words, employers can prove that age is an important, job-related criterion for job selection.

When older individuals feel they have been discriminated against on the basis of age, they can file a charge of discrimination. Initially, it is the employee's (or job candidate's) responsibility to assert a prima facie case of the age discrimination claim. In other words, the person filing the charge must show that the claim has some face validity by proving the following:

- The employee/job candidate is a member of the protected class (meets the age requirement of being older than forty).

- There was an adverse personnel action taken with respect to the older worker, such as less pay, termination, failure to hire, failure to promote.

- A younger, similarly situated employee was treated better.

- The older employee/job candidate was as good or as qualified as the younger individual.[11]

An apparent case of age discrimination would be if a company's hiring history demonstrated that it never hired anyone over forty.

Once the older employee/job candidate offers enough evidence to assert a case, then the employer is required to provide evidence that the actions were motivated by legitimate business reasons, unrelated to age. Once the employer shows evidence that the actions were nondiscriminatory, it is up to the older employee/job candidate to show that age was the determining factor in the action taken by the employer.

Employers may prove that they took action because of four reasons that are acceptable by the ADEA:

- There was good cause for termination.

- There was a bona fide occupational qualification.

- There were reasonable factors other than age that led to the employer's action.

- There was a bona fide seniority system or benefit plan necessitating the employer's actions.[12]

When an employer is proved to have been discriminatory, remedies can include back pay, reinstatement, and promotion, depending upon the discriminatory violation. Additionally, plaintiffs may also recover double damages if the violation was willful. However, punitive damages, as well as additional sums for emotional distress, have been disallowed.

The ADEA also provides for the right to a jury trial.

Prevalence of Age Discrimination

Age discrimination claims have proliferated in the past years. In 1981, the number of charges was about 12,700; in 1986, that number grew to over 26,500. There was a slight decrease in charges in 1987, declining to 24,900.[13]

Increased public awareness has been cited as one of the reasons for this increase, as has the broadening of ADEA since its enactment.[14] One report says the increase is caused by America's businesses making more age-related decisions, especially with increased downsizing and merger activities affecting more older workers.[14]

Not only are there more cases, but many of those cases are becoming more costly to the employer. In 1988, Westinghouse Inc. agreed to pay $35 million to about four thousand former employees in two age discrimination cases. It was the largest cash settlement in the history of the Equal Employment Opportunity Commission.[15]

Avoiding Discriminatory Practices

There are several ways in which an employer might inadvertently discriminate. However, if the actions are discriminatory, the employer nevertheless is in violation of ADEA. Some ways in which companies may inadvertently discriminate include:

- A belief that human resources depreciate over time, reflected in policies that encourage early retirement, or that favor the promotion or training of younger workers over older workers.

- A policy of mandatory retirement.

- A reduction in force in which the single criterion for layoff is age, seniority, or other age-oriented factors.

- Hiring policies that favor younger workers over older workers.

- Promotions, training, and retraining that offer preferential treatment to younger workers over older workers.

- Discharge of older workers, particularly when there are more discharges of older workers, or when younger workers are not discharged for the same infractions.

It is important for companies to realize that intent is not an ingredient in determining whether age discrimination is taking place; it is the result of the employer's action that is in question. Therefore, businesses must be certain their actions cannot be interpreted as being discriminatory.

What can employers do to ensure that inadvertent discrimination is not taking place? Some suggestions made by Patrick Nepute, a partner with the law firm of Greenebaum, Doll & McDonald in Louisville, Kentucky, are:

- Use targeted recruiting sources to attract older workers.

- Ensure that any mention of age in preemployment settings is eliminated. For example, references to age, birth date, and high school graduation date during the employment application and interview may be considered evidence of discrimination. Also, remove any references to "young men and women" in recruitment advertisements.

- Be consistent in the selection process, asking the same questions of all job candidates. For example, if physical strength is important in the job (such as the ability to lift twenty-five pounds or to stand for four hours), all job candidates should be asked questions that determine their physical limitations. If these questions are asked only of older candidates, then the question may be discriminatory.

- Use precautionary measures to protect against potential age discrimination claims by having written policies that forbid age discrimination or posters that state the company's policies on fair employment practices.

- Develop an orientation program that informs each new employee about employment practices and policies. At orientation, give each new employee a copy of the policy manual, and have that employee sign a statement acknowledging receipt.

- Use a step-by-step disciplinary action policy for employees who do not meet performance standards, or who fail to follow company policies and procedures. Be consistent in the application of this process, and keep written documentation for all disciplinary actions.

- Conduct regular (annual or more often) performance appraisals that accurately reflect the performance of all employees. Appraisals should be in writing.

- Larger employers should conduct a regular employment audit of all employment and human resources data, including employee demographic data, hire data, promotions, training, benefits, and so on. Companies should look not only at the numbers of older workers within the company and at the various levels within the organization, but also on the effect of practices.

Consider having a centralized office or department, preferably the human resources department, review any and all personnel decisions to ensure that they are consistent and free of age bias. The department would review each decision to ensure that each case is properly documented. It also would review all appraisals for accuracy and consistency.

Eliminating Ageism and Discrimination in the Workplace

Greeting cards, advertisements, and media messages do not necessarily depict the older American in the most favorable light. Calling older adults "over the hill" or "old buzzards" is less than complimentary. Some argue that this attitude means the American public is finally able to laugh about a phenomenon that was once filled with apprehension and dread—the fact of growing older. But, derogatory terms, even though said in jest, are in fact ageist. And, just as the workplace sought to eliminate language that might be labeled as sexist or racist, businesses must now seek to eliminate ageist language.

Acceptable terms to describe today's older adults include:

- senior citizens
- retired persons
- mature Americans
- elderly persons
- older Americans
- middle-aged persons
- golden-agers
- aged persons
- older persons/older man/older woman[16]

As explained in chapter 2, each term can connote a subset of the older population; therefore, care should be taken when using any of these terms. For example, a person in his late fifties probably would take offense at "senior citizen," or "elderly person," as these terms connote an individual that is much older.

Positive terms that describe older persons include:

- august
- experienced
- mature
- mellow
- sage
- seasoned
- veteran
- well-versed
- wise[17]

Again, while each of these terms is a positive one, care should be taken to ensure that it is appropriate given the individual and the circumstances.

Generally speaking, older persons like to be regarded as individuals, not as members of an "older" category. Therefore, they wish to be treated as other persons, and in the workplace, treated as other workers, without special treatment. To the degree possible, older workers should be mainstreamed in the workplace.

A primary goal of business today should be to eliminate ageism and age discrimination from the workplace. As has been discussed, age discrimination can be unintentional; yet if the effects of a personnel policy or action is discriminatory, then the company is held responsible. Ageism is a more pervasive evil, as it represents a negative stereotyping of older adults that may intentionally or unintentionally discourage older adults from remaining in the workplace, progressing within the work environment, or considering reentry into a second or third career.

Good business encourages the further employment of today's greatest resources: its older workers. Eliminating ageism and age discrimination will be a key factor in providing the right environment for these workers.

Managing for Retention of Older Workers

Increasing labor shortages means employers must be highly creative in offering a work environment that encourages older employees to stay on board. What can management do to ensure that experienced employees stay with the company? Here are seven questions that businesses should ask when trying to retain top senior employees.

Does the company reward employees for good performance? One of the top considerations experienced employees look for is recognition for good work. Increasingly, companies are adopting formal reward systems such as pay-for-performance programs, incentive programs, profit sharing, top performer awards, and service awards. Informal strategies, such as a memo saying "Thank you for a job well done," are also important in communicating that the efforts of employees are not being taken for granted.

Is fair treatment provided to all employees? Experienced workers want an environment they perceive to be fair and void of age discrimination and ageism. Some employers are responding by setting up internal boards of trained employees to handle grievances. Employers are also paying attention to ensure that fair, consistent measures are being used for all employees.

Do all employees have a chance for growth and development? Experienced workers, along with their younger counterparts, are looking for a chance to grow within the company. Therefore, it is important to make training programs readily available, and to make sure that older workers have equal access to these programs.

Does two-way communication exist in the company? Experienced workers want the freedom to speak their minds and give their opinions about daily business operations. Management can ease the way for open communications through frequent, informal contact with employees. More formal approaches, including an open-door policy and an older worker task force, can help by encouraging suggestions from this employee group.

Does job design take into account employees' needs? Qualities that experienced workers look for in a job include flexible scheduling, interesting and varied work, and the ability to see the results of their efforts.

Does the company demonstrate respect for all employees? Respect can be demonstrated in a number of ways, including fair and consistent management practices and concern for employees inside and outside the workplace.

Does the company permit a "fun" work environment? A study by a California university found that fun in the workplace can be a powerful personnel motivator that improves job performance.

Companies that value the talents and skills of older workers are taking a close look within their own doors to ensure that management policies and practices address these seven questions—and lead to a quality work environment for all workers, young and old alike.

Summary

To the extent that businesses are suffering from labor shortages and the baby bust, unqualified and unskilled job candidates, and less-than-productive workers, the solution to these problems may indeed lie with the increased employment of older workers. And, while additional recruitment of these workers may be one way to add experience to the workforce, the best method is to provide a work environment that is conducive to the effective employment of members of the aging workforce.

Employers need to work to understand the needs, values, and perspectives of older workers, and must remove barriers that have led to age discrimination and ageism. Programs and policies that retain workers must be a priority for organizations that want to continue to rely on the experience, talents, and maturity of the older worker.

Notes

1. See Morris Massey, *The People Puzzle*, Reston Publishing Company, Inc., Reston, Virginia, 1979, p. 181.
2. See "Managing a Changing Work Force." 1986, American Association of Retired Persons, p. 3.
3. Ibid., p. 1.
4. Ibid., pp. 2–3.
5. See "Hire Older Workers as Consultants to Fill Temporary Jobs, Consultant Suggests," *The Older Worker*, November 1988, p. 6.
6. See L. Wiener, "Your Home, The Office," *U.S. News and World Report*, September 26, 1988, pp. 64–66.
7. See "Managing a Changing Work Force." 1986, American Association of Retired Persons, p. 3.
8. See "How to Manage Older Workers," 1988, American Association of Retired Persons, p. 7.
9. See "1988 ASPA/CCH Survey," Commerce Clearing House, 1988, p. 3.
10. See "How to Manage Older Workers," 1988, American Association of Retired Persons, pp. 4–6.
11. See Patrick Nepute, "Age Discrimination," Louisville, Kentucky, 1989, p. 8.
12. Ibid., pp. 9–10.
13. See "America's Changing Work Force." American Association of Retired Persons, p. 12.
14. See "Questions and Answers: How Are Businesses Challenged by Age-Bias Suits?" *The Aging Workforce*, December 1987, pp. 1–3.

15. See "Case Settled for $35 Million," *The Older Worker*, August 1988, pp. 6–7.
16. See Frank Nuessel, "Ageist Language" *Maledicta* 8, 1984, pp. 17–28.
17. Ibid.

7
Retirement and the Aging
Work Force

A society that gives to one class all the opportunities for leisure, and to another all the burdens of work, dooms both classes to spiritual sterility.

—Lewis Mumford

Retired is being tired twice, I've thought,
First tired of working,
Then tired of not.
—Richard Armour

In today' society it is considered a privilege, an honor, and a blessing to be able to retire. Many Americans spend considerable time thinking about when they won't have to work any more; in fact, just listen in any corporate lunchroom and you are bound to hear conversations about what individuals would be doing if they were retired. Retirement is considered to be something that is earned by years of working hard and doing what is expected. It is the pot of gold at the end of the rainbow.

Americans are heading in droves for the pot of gold, and are retiring at earlier ages. In 1955, for example, 65 percent of men older than fifty-five were working; in 1980 this figure dropped to 46 percent. For men sixty-five to sixty-nine, 57 percent were employed in 1955, compared with only 28.5 percent in 1980. Statistics show that labor force participation rates for men have continually dropped through the 1980s. For women, the decline in participation rates has not been as dramatic; however, recent data dem-

onstrate that women also are retiring early more frequently.[1]

Why are more workers retiring early? Is retirement always the best option? How should employers help them
plan for retirement? What should be included in a successful preretirement planning program? These are some of the
issues discussed in this chapter.

Why the Early Retirement Trend?

There is definitely a trend toward early retirement, caused
in part by its social acceptance. A number of other factors
also contribute:

- Many older workers cannot find work because of low
  skill levels, or because of discrimination in the workplace. As a result, they get discouraged, quit looking for
  work, and become "retired."

- With many companies undergoing downsizing and merger activity, lucrative early retirement packages are being offered to senior employees, who are opting for this
  "golden handshake."

- Physically demanding work, causes some older workers
  to burn out.

- Disability or health problems cause some older workers
  to choose retirement.

- Children, other family members, and friends pressure
  them to "take it easy" and to do the accepted thing.

Retirement may not be the best decision. Even though
more older workers are retiring, many are unhappy with
their decision. Why is retirement not always the best option? Consider the following:

- An individual may be unable to meet basic financial obligations because of a small or nonexistent pension, low Social Security benefits, and no additional income source.

- Persons may get bored with retirement because they never developed hobbies or never thought about how to spend all that leisure time.

- Older individuals may get lonely, and mis￢ ￢he social network at work.

- An individual may miss the mental stimulation and professional challenge of the work environment.

Whether it is one of these reasons, or a host of others, many retirees are finding themselves totally unprepared for the world of leisure, either financially, emotionally, or socially. Successful retirement requires careful planning, and, for many older individuals, planning for a combination of work and leisure.

Planning for Retirement

Some older workers take responsibility for their own retirement planning, attending courses held at their community college on the subject, talking with friends, spouses, and children about retirement planning, or even hiring a professional, often an accountant and an attorney, to assist in the planning process.

Increasingly, companies are providing their older workers with a preretirement planning program. Programs include seminars, booklets and other informational materials, and even retirement rehearsals.

What activities are being successfully conducted by businesses? How are these plans being implemented? What services are available to help employers develop preretirement sessions?

NCOA's Retirement Planning Program. The National Council on the Aging (NCOA) has developed a retirement planning program for employers. Companies including Merck, Atlantic Richfield, Travelers, and Alcoa are working with NCOA in implementing retirement planning as part of the employee benefit program. More than seventy-five corporations use this program.

NCOA's program permits employers to select the option most compatible with the company's needs. The company can have NCOA coach the company's management on the program, invite NCOA to do the training, or purchase the materials from NCOA.

The twenty-hour program covers: lifestyle planning, financial planning, health, interpersonal relationships, living arrangements, and leisure and work options. It uses a multimedia approach for ease in learning, as well as group exercises and individual exercises.

Each program is tailored for the company and its needs. Companies can include very specific corporate information, such as employee benefits. Businesses interested in learning more should contact the director of Corporate Programs for NCOA (refer to the appendix for contact information).[2]

Community resources for retirement planning. In many communities, hospitals are developing resource centers for health and retirement planning. In Louisville, Kentucky, for example, Jewish Hospital has developed the Jewish Hospital Health and Information Center. The center is a community library offering these services and information:.

- An extensive array of books, journals, magazines, and videotapes on aging and retirement planning

- Health checks and screenings by health care professionals
- A mall walking program
- Health seminars, lifestyle and retirement planning seminars, insurance counseling, and community resources information.

The center is one of twenty-four in the nation, developed in connection with Age Wave, Inc., and Ken Dychtwald, Ph.D. of Emeryville, California.[3]

"Feeling Fine" program on wellness. In Little Rock, Arkansas, the Arkansas Business Health Coalition and the University of Arkansas at Little Rock have developed a program for preretirement planning. Called Feeling Fine, the program focuses on health promotion and wellness, a perspective that many preretirement programs do not emphasize as much as is often needed.

The modular program offers topics on health and aging, lifestyle and wellness, change and adjustment, resources, housing, financial management, insurance, legal issues, long-term care, and death and dying.

Employers can purchase the program for about forty dollars per set of booklets. Betty Wood, a planning specialist for the program, sees this as a way for employers to cut their retiree health costs, while offering a much-needed benefit to employees.[4]

"Rehearsing" retirement. Despite all the planning tools in the world, it is still hard for many older workers to imagine what life will be like without work. To help these older workers test the waters, one company is experimenting with "rehearsal retirement."

Kollmorgen Corporation's Electro-Optical Division in Northampton, Massachusetts, lets older employees work part time with the company, then donate time to a community agency. The program begins one year before the intended retirement date, with employees volunteering their time at an approved non-profit agency. Initially, employees work three days at the company and two days at the agency; after eight months, workers spend two days at the company and three days at the agency.

There are many winners in Kollmorgen's program. The agency benefits because it gets extra help. The company benefits because it has ample time to replace the retiring employees. The company often promotes from within, and this one-year period allows an opportunity to assess the competence of several individuals. Also, the soon-to-be-retiring employee can provide training to the replacement. The firm is recognized within the community as a good corporate citizen. The retiring employee wins, having had the chance to see how a reduced work schedule will impact lifestyle and other issues. The employee receives full pay, benefits, and pension accruals, so there is no risk.

The program is relatively easy to administer, with little additional paperwork.

Polaroid Corporation in Cambridge, Massachusetts, also offers its older workers an opportunity to try out retirement with an unpaid three-month leave. Additionally, the company provides a "tapering off" program, which permits employees to gradually cut hours before retirement. Employees are paid only for hours worked, but receive full medical insurance and prorated pension credits.[5]

Links with community services. In Woodland Hills, California, one company has found that by working with other local businesses it can provide comprehensive preretirement planning for its employees. Data Products Corporation has developed partnerships with a local hospital, bank, and law firm to establish an annual comprehensive planning program for employees.

Such partnership companies often are willing to provide this service free, as it gives them an opportunity to promote their businesses to employees attending the session. Data Products works closely with seminar leaders to ensure that the program is on target for the participants. Employees have the chance to evaluate each presenter, permitting Data Products to modify the program as needed.

The session is usually attended by employees fifty to sixty-four, and lasts about six weeks. Subjects are on nutrition, diet, money management, and insurance. The course has been enthusiastically attended by employees, and costs the company little.[6]

Software programs to aid retirement planning. For companies that want to provide workers with assistance in finding the right geographic location for retirement, a new software package can help. The program is called RETIRE, and helps match older persons with cities that meet their needs. It was developed by Robert Borden of Martlet Inc., based in Herndon, Virginia.

Individuals enter into the system such information as climate preferences, lifestyle choices, health status, and other pertinent data. The program generates listings of the 430 cities within the system that meet those specific needs.

The cost of the program is nominal; a monthly fee of seventy-nine dollars is charged to businesses; thirty-nine dollars to individuals.[7]

The Corporate Retirees Network. Some employers want to provide their retiring seniors with a network of other seniors. That community service may be available nationwide in the near future. In the northwest, there is already such a system, called the Corporate Retirees Network.

The network is the nation's first association of employer-based retiree programs that consists of postretirement groups or clubs focusing on reemployment, health and fitness, volunteer service, and other issues. The network places seniors in paid or volunteer work, provides retirement planning information, and strengthens the retirement planning programs in existence in corporate America.

The network has sponsored workshops for strengthening corporate retirement programs, has published a newsletter, and has provided technical assistance for employers. It also has conducted a survey to be published in *Retirees— Hidden Assets.*[8]

Companies may find that by developing such partnerships they are better able to provide these services easily and affordably to their retiring workers.

Postretirement assistance. While many companies are offering preretirement planning services to senior employees, some companies are also providing assistance once the employee has retired. This service is of great benefit to employees who may have felt they didn't need to plan, or who thought they knew what they wanted to do. When retirement became a reality, however, priorities and needs change, and these retirees need help.

The Travelers, a leader in addressing the needs of an aging population, has added a postretirement program to assist its retired employees. The sponsor is Senior Job Bank, a nonprofit community service agency based in Travelers' hometown city of Hartford, Connecticut. The program's mission is to provide job counseling and placement for persons fifty-five and older.

The five-day, fifteen-hour program is provided three times a year. Sessions are limited to twenty people, and there is a small fee for attending. Topics include how to find a job and what options are available, including volunteer positions and educational opportunities.[9]

Planning and Implementing
a Preretirement Program

What should an employer consider when planning and implementing a preretirement planning program?

Bonnie Maitlen, president of B.R. Maitlen and Associates, a consulting and training program that specializes in personal and professional development, including preretirement planning, gives some advice. After conducting several preretirement planning seminars, she has consistently heard similar feedback from the seminar participants:

- "I wish I had started earlier in this process . . . now there are fewer financial planning options for me since I am just now beginning to plan for my retirement."

- "I didn't remember everything that I was told in my last days on the job. Those were very emotional days for me, and I wish that the information had been given to me before the process."

- "I had given no thought at all to retirement planning until my employer offered a seminar to us. I am so happy that I have had this time to prepare for my 'golden years.' "

- "It was great that my company offered me the preretirement planning seminar, and that my spouse was invited. It gave us the opportunity to talk through some issues we had never discused before and to make some mutual decisions."

- "I had no idea that there were so many options and decisions to make! It was great to have an expert present to help us make those important plans."

In general, Maitlen feels that it is a plus when companies

offer preretirement planning, since it is a much-needed employee benefit that can be added very cost-effectively.

Preretirement Planning Program Content

Some basic topics included in most programs are: health, fitness, and wellness; financial planning and money management; legal issues; benefit and pension programs; lifestyle, housing, and values; work and volunteerism.

In preparing a retirement planning guide for Lee Hecht Harrison, Inc., Maitlen discovered that the retirees of one of her larger clients appreciated the section on work options. In this section, Maitlen explores such issues as:

- Identification of skills and abilities that may be put to use in similar or different paid or volunteer work settings;

- Evaluation of the labor market, including an analysis of work options, such as part time, full time, volunteerism, and entrepreneurship;

- How-to information on preparing a résumé, cover letter, biographical data sheet, and other job-search tools;

- How-to information on business plans, networking to find the desired work, and other employment skills.

Maitlen says that, initially, most older workers felt this section was not very useful, since their thoughts were on retirement, not on work. However, Maitlen reports that many participants came back to her in later sessions to say that work information was one of the most essential areas. For employers eager to entice workers to remain active in the workplace, this is an important section to include. Older adults, who are more active and healthy today than ever before, will increasingly seek work options.

Formatting the Preretirement Program

What should a preretirement program look like? How long should it last? How should it be structured?

Ideally, the preretirement planning program should be presented in sections over time. It is unrealistic to think that so much information can be squeezed into a one day program.

Plan four to ten sections for relaying information. Each section can focus on a particular issue and cover it in some depth. Employers planning to use community services or outside consultants to present some of the information will find this structure particularly helpful.

By spreading the information out over time, retiring workers can give some thought to the issues and come to the next session with followup questions. This process permits the use of take-home exercises that give the employee an opportunity for personal reflection and spouse input.

Many companies have found that including the spouse in retirement planning seminars is a good idea. Since many retirement decisions will be made jointly, it is helpful if the spouse can be present to hear information from the experts. When spouses are present, courses can be designed to include dyad exercises.

The group environment can be an important element of the planning seminar, Maitlen reports. She finds that often a validation process occurs when seniors hear about shared fears, concerns, and issues. She knows there is value in processing information together as a group, but cautions that some information, especially financial, is highly personal. Confidentiality is often required to ensure maximum effectiveness.

There is also some value in mixing group sessions with one-on-one counseling. In many cases, individuals and couples may want to talk with the seminar leader about personal matters or unusual circumstances.[10]

Summary

Retirement planning is a relatively new benefit, but increasingly, companies are offering it. It is a relatively cost-effective benefit. With new services, agencies, consultants, and organizations now offering these services to businesses, employers should put themselves in a position to make available a planning program that meets employees' needs.

Notes

1. See "32 Million Older Americans: A Handbook for Employers on the Trends, Issues, Laws, and Strategies Pertaining to Older Worker Utilization," The National Urban League, Inc., p. 9.
2. See "Helping Your Employees Plan For Retirement," *The Aging Workforce*, December 1987, p. 7.
3. See "Are You Planning To Retire?" *Choices for a Healthy Lifestyle*, Summer 1989, pp. 6–7.
4. See "Preretirement Planning Program Focuses on Health and Wellness," *The Older Worker*, October 1988, p. 8.
5. See "Companies Allow Older Workers A Chance to 'Rehearse' Retirement," *The Older Worker*, August 1988, pp. 2–3.
6. See "Firm Links With Community Services To Conduct Preretirement Planning," *The Older Worker*, July 1988, p. 4.
7. See "Software Helps Aged Find Places to Retire," *The Older Worker*, August 1988, p. 5.
8. See "The Newest Network: Corporate Retirees," *Aging Network News*, October 1989, p. 9.
9. See "HRM Update: Retiree Job Help," *The Personnel Administrator*, pp. 14–16.
10. Interview with Bonnie R. Maitlen.

8
Putting Experience to Work: Models in Employing Older Workers

Nothing can take the place of practical experience out in the world.
—A.B. Zu Tavern

The work force is aging, and today's businesses, if they are to remain productive and efficient, will begin to examine the issue of increased employment of older workers, by either attracting more of these workers, keeping them within the corporation in full-time positions, or by working with them to find alternate solutions that make sense within the corporation.

Companies interested in more fully utilizing the aging work force will research a variety of solutions to staffing problems, including the use of outside services, agencies, organizations, and consultants who can assist in making the transition from a youth-oriented work force to one that is focused on the needs and concerns of the aging employee population. Businesses will also begin to plan and strategize to build internal support structure for the increased employment of older workers.

What companies are successful in employing older workers? How are they redesigning the workplace to make increased employment of older workers a reality? What services, profit and nonprofit, assist employers in their efforts? What internal strategies should organizations implement in order to put more experience—in the form of older employees—to work? These questions are addressed in this chapter, focusing on successful models of employment of older workers.

Corporate Solutions: Putting Experience to Work

With corporate America recognizing the need to remain productive in a global economy, keeping the aging work force productive and effective is a top priority. Several corporations have already developed some excellent strategies to respond to needs of the aging work force, and to the staffing problems plaguing many businesses.

Here are some of the corporations that are taking a lead in attracting and keeping experienced workers:

- **Grumman Aerospace Company** in Bethpage, New York, works hard to retain its experienced workers because it is difficult and costly to gain security clearance for new employees.

- **Bankers Life and Casualty** in Chicago, Illinois, has created a pool of retired temporary workers to meet its ongoing need for temporary labor, saving the company ten thousand dollars in just one year.

- **Walt Disney World Company** in Lake Buena Vista, Florida, employs older workers in about 9 percent of its positions throughout the organization.

- **Control Data Corporation** in Minneapolis, Minnesota, has developed a new business advisers division that is made up of its retired professionals. Employees from this division are hired by other firms as independent consultants.

- **Good People** in New York City, **Senior Power,** based in Louisville, Kentucky, and **Retiree Skills Inc.** in Tucson, Arizona are temporary agencies that deal exclusively with older individuals because of the growing demand for experienced temporary workers.

- **Kelly Services,** based in Troy, Michigan, has met the growing demands for temporary workers by tapping the labor market of older workers.

- **Hardee's Food Systems, Inc.,** headquartered in Rocky Mount, North Carolina, **Kentucky Fried Chicken,** based in Louisville, Kentucky, and other quick-service restaurants are turning to the older worker as one means to meet the labor shortages caused by the baby bust.

- **Andy Frain Communications** in Chicago, Illinois—a company in the crowd control business—finds that older workers are much better at public security screening than their younger counterparts.

- **Builders Emporium,** headquartered in Irvine, California, finds that older workers not only understand customer service issues better than younger workers, but they also come from a do-it-yourself generation that makes their employment a natural fit.

- **Joseph Horn Department Store** in Pittsburgh, Pennsylvania, where unemployment is high, still prefers older workers, and has its hourly positions staffed with 32 percent older workers.

- **Wal-Mart Stores, Inc.,** based in Arkansas, employs older workers because they are an important part of the company's future growth.[1,2]

The list could go on and on with examples of companies that have recognized that the aging work force is a reality, and that knows that taking a leadership role means attracting and retaining more older workers.

Redesigning Work for the Aging Work Force

Employers are recognizing that to make the work force more attractive to older workers, they must make changes. While every company will have varying circumstances and conditions requiring tailoring and fine-tuning, here is what some innovative companies have done to make the increased employment of experienced workers a success.

Best Western. In Sun City, Arizona, the Best Western Hotel managers recognized that there was a good potential for recruiting more older workers for a variety of positions. They were disappointed with the quality of the younger workers who had been hired, unsuccessfully, for these positions.

Nils Kindgren, vice president of Newmark, Inc., the hotel management agent, saw a need to rethink the jobs and the corresponding recruitment messages if more senior employees were to be attracted to the jobs.

The first step was to change the recruitment messages, and to let older adults know that Best Western was looking for professionals, not just clerks. They began to stress that the hotel wanted and valued experience, and that the positions to be filled were responsible ones, because the employees came in direct contact with the customer. Job titles were redefined to carry the importance of the role. "Front desk clerks" became "ambassadors."

Redesign went a lot further than just cosmetic changes, however. Added flexibility was granted to the older workers who needed it, and managers found replacements when senior employees requested time off for health or personal reasons. Older workers were paid above the median salary for industry standards, and received health benefits as well.

The hotel management is pleased with the older workers, because they are particularly adept at providing excellent service to customers and upholding the hotel's high quality standards. Also, since a majority of the customers are older adults as well, it makes good business sense to have older workers serving these guests.[3]

Kelly Services. To meet a growing demand for its services, Kelly Services is aggressively recruiting older workers to take temporary positions with this national temporary help service. But to recruit enough workers to meet this need, the company had to go a lot further than just placing help-wanted advertisements in the newspaper.

The first step was to develop a national initiative to attract experienced workers. The program is called Encore, and offers the fifty-five-plus worker a supportive, flexible, friendly environment. Kelly conducted job fairs, worked with a variety of agencies and organizations that support the employment of older workers, and distributed information at branch offices. As of an October 1988 report, fifty thousand seniors had enrolled in Encore.

Kelly offers the kind of work environment older workers want, and maintains it by conducting focus groups with its current employees. It also receives updated information from national older worker organizations, such as the American Association of Retired Persons and the American Society on Aging.[4]

Honeywell Corporation. The Honeywell Corporation in Minneapolis, Minnesota, has gone the extra mile in providing the kind of workplace that is compatible with the needs and concerns of its older employees. It accomplishes this through an advisory committee composed of all the company's fifty-plus workers. The group is called the Older Workers League (OWL).

The league has existed since 1984, and attracts more than 20 percent of the company's senior employees. Twenty employees make up a governing council. OWL performs a number of responsibilities, including the review of issues of concern to older workers. It is also involved in the company's preretirement planning process.

OWL receives eighty thousand dollars a year to implement its activities, and Honeywell contributes employee time to participate in OWL activities. Thus far, the group's accomplishments include the sponsorship of symposiums, briefings on retirement information, and participation in a senior citizens' fair.

The group also plans to investigate more part-time employment as an option to retirement, increased benefit choices, and the company communications on retirement.[5]

Services to Assist in the Employment of Older Workers

Many companies are realizing that outside help and resources are needed to meet their needs of accommodating an aging work force. While some businesses need education and information, others need hands-on assistance in recruitment and retraining, and others need ideas to help recruit and retain older workers.

Many services are offered to employers today in the form of community partnerships and task forces, consultants, government-funded employment and training programs, and others. Examine some of the ways in which these programs and services are assisting employers in meeting their goals of increased employment of older workers.

Community task force. In Trenton, New Jersey, where labor shortages are the norm, companies are discovering that they need to do as much to retain their experienced workers as they do to recruit new workers. To help businesses focus more effectively on retention of older workers, the state has initiated a New Jersey Older Worker Task Force.

The task force offers a series of workshops for management and human resources professionals that covers topics on the facts of aging, how to manage an aging work force, providing benefits for older workers, and legal issues, including age discrimination. A manual has been developed and is distributed through local chambers of commerce.

The task force is composed of business leaders and older worker programs. Ongoing plans are to continue to provide education and specifically address issues of supervisory skills training for young managers.[6]

Employer Challenge Initiative. In the Boston area, where unemployment is low and finding workers is difficult, there is a real opportunity to reach out to older adults by using some creative approaches. The state has developed the Employer Challenge Initiative, providing grants to place older workers with employers, and to provide education and information to employers on older worker issues.

Some of the creative recruiting approaches that are being explored include offering competitive salaries, offering transportation reimbursements, redesigning monotonous jobs, and recruiting teams of older adults to work together. Creative solutions are also being explored to retain these workers, including expanded benefit packages, job sharing, tuition reimbursements for grandchildren, summer leaves without pay, and part-time work options.

One grant was given to Operation ABLE of Greater Boston, which has developed Impact 2000, a program that involves contracts with employers that pledge to provide employment opportunities to older workers.[7]

Making it Work: Putting Experience Back to Work

In order successfully to organize and implement a plan to employ and manage an aging workforce effectively, businesses need to begin making strategy plans now to address these issues. What should companies do to encourage the employment of older workers? How should businesses change in order to meet the needs of an aging workforce? Here are seven strategies that any business should begin to implement now to gain its fair share of the best employees that comprise this labor market segment.

1. Get educated! The needs and concerns of the aging work force are different from the needs and concerns of yesterday's work force. As has been discussed in this book, strategies to recruit and select, train, compensate, manage, and retire older workers are different for this new labor market segment. Companies need to look for ways to stay updated on aging issues that will affect the management of these workers.

What should employers do to remain updated on the information concerning older worker issues? Some suggestions for keeping abreast of the changing body of knowledge on these topics are:

• Read publications and information bulletins published by national older worker organizations, such as the American Association of Retired Persons, the National Council on Aging, and the National Urban League. Review the appendix in this book to identify organizations that provide newletters and other publications that give current information.

- Attend seminars and conferences conducted by national older worker organizations, and by other management and employment associations.

- Read *Modern Maturity* and other magazines tailored to the aging population.

- Talk with employers who have successfully targeted and employed older workers. Form a task force in the community with these employers to share information and success stories.

- Attend a college course on gerontology or on aging issues.

- Join a local task force on employing older workers, or one of the national organizations that supports the employment of older workers.

- Hire a consultant to provide the organization with tailored research and information on older workers issues.

- Ask current older workers to provide information on concerns and needs.

2. Analyze local, regional, and national resources. Many employers do not realize that there are myriad outside resources to provide information, guidance, and counseling on older worker issues. To identify these resources, employers may wish to:

- Review the organizations listed in the appendix, then call or write to let these organizations know of the company's interest in providing more opportunities to employ older workers. Ask the organizations how they can help.

- Look in the phone book for local organizations that provide services for employers. Look under the key words *senior, older workers,* and *employment.*

- Call the local Private Industry Council (PIC) or the local Jobs Training Partnership Act (JTPA) office for information on local services for employment of older workers.

- Contact the local or state employment service office to discover what services may be provided for recruiting and training older workers.

- Network with area employers to determine what services are helpful in finding and training older workers.

- Call the local college to determine which professors on campus understand employment issues for older workers, or gerontological issues.

3. Gain total management support. The effectiveness of many corporate programs can be measured immediately by the degree of involvement, commitment, and support by top management. The initiative to respond to the needs of an aging work force demands high-level involvement.

How do department managers, first-line supervisors, and others communicate the needs of an aging work force to top management? How does one gain the support and commitment from the total management team? Some guidelines for gaining that support from all levels of management include:

- Keep top management informed on changing demographics, labor shortages, and the need to respond to an aging work force. Accomplish this through "white paper" reports, human resource strategy reports, human resource "audits," clippings of important newspaper and trade journal articles, and by providing a copy of this book!

- Form a task force that includes representatives from all levels of management to address aging work force issues. Be sure to gain an understanding of any resistance to increased employment of older workers.

- Include management issues relating to an aging work force in performance evaluations. Management tunes in to the importance of these issues when pay is linked to behavior.

- Develop a corporate strategy aimed at recruiting, selecting, training, compensating, managing, retaining, and retiring older workers. Involve as many layers of the management team as possible.

- Communicate to all employees achievement of corporate goals in increased employment/retention of older workers.

4. Eliminate barriers to the employment of older workers. There are a great many barriers, internal and external, that prohibit employment of older workers within the corporate environment. Internal barriers include age discrimination or the more subtle ageism, inflexible work options, and outdated job designs, personnel policies, and procedures. External barriers are perceptions that the organization does not want to employ older workers, or recruitment messages that do not reach the older adult.

What steps can a company take to remove these barriers to employment? How can a company make the necessary changes to ensure increased employment? Consider the following guidelines:

- Conduct a complete human resources audit to determine if any policy or procedure, from recruitment, selection, training, or compensation, to managing, retirement, or termination, includes any practice that results in an action that discriminates against (or has a negative effect on) older employees. Immediately modify any negative policy or procedure to ensure age-neutral policies.

- Look closely to see if flexibility can be added to job scheduling. Investigate options being offered by other companies, and evaluate the opportunities to incorporate these options internally.

- Evaluate job redesign issues that will accommodate more older workers. Ask current older workers how jobs could be made more responsive to the needs and concerns of the older worker.

- Analyze recruitment messages and other external communications regarding employment. Include older workers in group pictures of employees. Use targeted approaches to appeal to older job candidates.

5. Implement methods to attract and retain older workers. The increased and effective employment of an aging work force doesn't just happen. It comes about from careful planning that incorporates an understanding of the desires of older adults.

What steps should an organization take to more effectively attract and retain workers?

- Attract older workers by using targeted recruitment approaches that let them know they are wanted in the job. Use targeted messages in places where older adults conduct daily activities.

- Attract and retain older workers by meeting their needs. Provide flexibility in work schedules, jobs that are redesigned to accommodate older workers' needs, and an environment free of ageism.

- Use resources that assist in the employment and training of older workers. Refer to the appendix for employment and training programs that work with employers and older workers.

- Re-examine compensation policies, training programs, performance evaluations, and other management tools within the corporation. Ensure that these tools are effective in providing for the needs of an aging work force.

6. *Train supervisors for managing a changing and aging work force.* Managers today are largely unprepared for the challenges of supervising a diverse older work force. They need additional training.

- Offer in-house training programs tailored to the specific needs of the corporation that deal with value systems, needs and concerns, ageism and age discrimination, motivation, and other aging issues.

- Send first-line supervisors to outside training seminars on the topics of managing for a diverse/aging workforce.

- Develop an in-house newsletter for managers that updates them on aging issues.

- Include management personnel on task forces for addressing older worker concerns.

7. *Keep communication lines open.* Listening and responding to employee issues remains one of the most important steps a company can take in increasing productivity and morale. Here are some specific methods for effectively communicating with employees:

- Develop a task force of older workers to discuss ways the company can better meet the evolving needs of an aging work force. Form an "older workers league" to let older employees know that their concerns are a priority.

- Get employees involved in designing benefit programs, training plans, and other management issues. The more employees are involved, the more they feel a commitment to the organization.

- Use attitude surveys to listen to employees' opinions about the work environment. Use surveys on a regular basis to understand how issues are evolving.

- Invite employees to ask questions during company meetings. Use a fifty-fifty format, in which 50 percent of the time is spent covering management issues, and 50 percent is spent answering employee questions.

- Practice "management by wandering around." Walk out in the shop, office, and other job sites, and talk with employees about the job. Ask questions like, "How can we make this a better place to work?" and "What could we do to make you more satisfied with your employment here?"

- Plan meetings with small groups of employees to discuss issues of concern. Make these meetings informal, and encourage employees to raise questions that are important to them.

- Adopt an open-door policy, and ask that all employees come to any level of management with questions or problems. Protect employees who want anonymity. Treat all questions with confidentiality.

- Respond when problems or questions are raised. It's not enough just to listen—in fact, employee morale can deteriorate when employees feel that management doesn't care about employee concerns. Devise a feedback system to let employees know what employee issues are being addressed, what items will be addressed in the near future, and what issues will not be acted upon immediately and why. Communicate action items and goal achievement through employee newsletters, employee meetings, and informal systems.

Brainpower and Talent

Many corporations believe mandatory retirement was a tremendous waste of the talent and experience of the older worker. One individual who felt strongly about what the older worker could offer and achieve was Colonel Harland Sanders, founder of Kentucky Fried Chicken Corporation, who made this statement before a U.S. Congressional Committee on Aging, May 25, 1977:

Representative Pepper and members of the committee, thank you for inviting me to give you my views on forced retirement.

I'm dead against it. Folks shouldn't be forced to retire just because they're sixty-five—or any other age. Folks should be allowed to work as long as they want to and as long as they can do the job. The role God gave Adam in the Garden of Eden was not that he should work until retirement age, but "till thou return unto the ground."

We older folks can have a lot to contribute.

Take Benjamin Franklin. He was seventy years old when he was appointed to the committee that wrote the Declaration of Independence, and he got France to recognize the United States when he was seventy-two. Probably his greatest contribution to this country came when he was eighty-one years old. That's when he almost single-handedly got the factions of Congress—there are always factions, aren't there—to compromise on our Constitution, and then he helped get it ratified.

It was a good thing that he hadn't been forced to

retire. We might not have had a country or a constitution.

Thomas Jefferson brought about the founding of the University of Virginia when he was seventy-six.

Thomas Alva Edison kept inventing things long after his sixty-fifth birthday. George C. Marshall was sixty-seven when he designed the European Recovery Program, for which he received the Nobel Prize.

Those are dramatic examples.

There are a lot more folks who have contributed in more common ways, and many who continue to contribute. Now it's not that us older folks are smarter than you youngsters, but at least we've had an opportunity to make most of the common mistakes. We've had our quota of disappointments and burned fingers. We've lost some of the fears and insecurities that plagued our youth. And, to the degree that we've learned from these experiences, we've gained some wisdom.

I'm not against retirement for people who want it. But retirement's just not for me. I believe a man will rust out quicker'n he'll wear out. I'm an 1890 model, and I'm planning to work another thirteen years and then become a senior citizen.

I don't want to quit working. Sitting in a rocker has never appealed to me. And golf or fishing isn't as much fun as working. Even if we can afford it, we should not rely on loafing. Life does not have to be easy to be wonderful. Retirement should merely mean we stop doing one thing and start doing something else. We should wish to get up every morning with the feeling that we have something to do, or perhaps not as a means of livelihood, but for our physical health and mental welfare and our happiness. We've got to keep our eye on what's coming up, not what's slipping by.

As you know, I really didn't get started on franchising Kentucky Fried Chicken until I was sixty-six—after I'd been forced to sell my restaurant because the interstate bypassed the place I'd been operating for twenty-five years. Now there are more than six thousand

Kentucky Fried Chicken restaurants around the world, selling about a billion meals a year and providing jobs for about one hundred thousand folks.

I'm proud of what I started, and I travel about a quarter of a million miles a year making sure the stores are run right, because my name's on them.

I love going around to stores teaching the young folks and raising a little hell once in a while when things aren't going exactly right. I'm a one-man consumer protection agency. When I work, I forget my little aches and pains. When I'm *really* busy, I forget I ever had an ache.

There are lots of folks like me. Working is their hobby. They like staying active, facing real business challenges. And some people past sixty-five need to work, they need the money. Inflation eats up their savings at a time when they've reached an expensive part of life—when there are more doctor and hospital bills than usual. I've had so many older people tell me that they never thought of inflation before they retired. And now they have slim pickin's.

Retirement's all right for those who like it, who have other interests to keep them physically and mentally active, and who have the money to afford it. But we shouldn't force retirement on everybody.

It would almost seem that retirement could be taken like a doctor's prescription—a simple following of instructions. But it is not so.

We're wasting a lot of brainpower and energy by making people retire. I'd like to see it stopped.

And one other thing, letting people work past age sixty-five might help keep the Social Security system from going broke!

Thank you for allowing me to appear.

As the Colonel said, the practice of forced retirement was a waste of a lot of brainpower and energy. But not allowing opportunities for older workers to continue to contribute to the work force is equally a waste of talent and manpower.

Today's businesses must seek methods to make the continued employment of its aging work force a meaningful, productive, and positive one. Today's work force is indeed coming of age. Smart business leaders will begin to initiate strategies to make the effective employment of older workers a solution to many of the changes taking place in the work force today.

Notes

1. See Sondra K. Match, "A New Look at Companies That Hire Experience," *Perspective on Aging*, September/October 1987, pp. 18–20.
2. See Lawrence S. Root, Ph.D., "Corporate Programs for Older Workers," *Aging*, No. 351, 1985, p. 12.
3. See "Best Western Increases Job Duties To Attract Responsible Senior Workers." *The Older Worker*, pp. 1–2.
4. See "Kelly Lures Older People Back To Work With the Benefits of Temporary Employment." *The Older Worker*, October 1988, pp. 1–2.
5. See "Honeywell Stays on Top of Employees' Concerns With Older Workers League." *The Older Worker*, October 1988, p. 2.
6. See "N.J. Task Force Helps Companies Put a 'Tourniquet' on Their Internal Workforce," *The Older Worker*, November 1988, p. 7.
7. See "Mass. Employer Challenge Helps Firms Looking For older Workers " *The Older Worker*, January 1989, pp. 6–7.

Appendix: Contact Information for Older Worker Organizations

AMERICAN ASSOCIATION OF RETIRED PERSONS
1909 K Street, N.W.
Washington, D.C. 20049
Association telephone number: (202) 872-4700
Contact: Glenn Northup, National Project Director, Senior Community Services Employment Program, (202) 662-4800
Contact: David Gamse, Worker Equity Program, (202) 662-4956
Contact: Jan Davidson, NOWIS, (202) 728-4896

AARP's Senior Community Services Employment Program has 108 locations in thirty-three states and in Puerto Rico. AARP's Worker Equity Initiative's mission is to foster attitudes, practices, and policies on work and retirement to meet the needs of a changing and aging work force.

The National Older Workers Information System (NOWIS) is a computerized data base of hundreds of older worker employment programs in place in private sector companies. Maintained by AARP, NOWIS is available as a resource for employers, unions, and other groups interested in learning innovative ways to utilize the skills and experience of older workers.

The publication *Workers Over 50: Old Myths, New Realities* is published by AARP and is available through the AARP office. Many other publications by Worker Equity are available upon request, including *Using the Experience of a Lifetime* and the newsletter *Working Age*.

Ageline is a data base produced and maintained by AARP.

NATIONAL URBAN LEAGUE, INC.
500 East 62nd Street
New York, New York 10021
Telephone: (212) 310-9201
Contact: Janet Zobel, National Program Director, Seniors in Community Service Program.

The National Urban League is an interracial, nonprofit community service organization that uses the tools and methods of education, social work, economics, law, business management, and other disciplines to secure equal opportunities in all sectors of society for African-Americans and other low-income persons.

The National Urban League operates in 113 cities in thirty-four states and the District of Columbia. The Seniors in Community Service Program (SCSP) operated programs for older adults through twenty-four affiliates in twenty-seven communities. *32 Million Older Workers: A handbook for employers on the trends, issues, laws, and strategies pertaining to older worker utilization* was published by the National Urban League.

NATIONAL COUNCIL ON THE AGING, INC.
600 Maryland Avenue, S.W.
West Wing 100
Washington, D.C. 20024
Telephone: (202) 479-1200
Contact: Don Davis, Vice-President, Division of Community Services Employment.
Contact: Joyce Welsh, Project Director, Prime Time Productivity Program

The National Council on the Aging, Inc., founded in 1950, is a national, nonprofit organization dedicated to the principle that the nation's older people are entitled to lives of dignity, security, and physical, mental, and social well-being and to full participation in society.

Publications, 1989 is a listing of publications available through the NCOA, including many on age and employment.

Perspective on Aging is a bimonthly magazine offered by NCOA through membership.

Current Literature on Aging is a quarterly, annotated bibliography.

The **National Association of Older Worker Employment Services** is an affiliate group of NCOA. It is the only older worker/employment membership group in the country. NCOA members can join one affiliate group free of charge.

The **Prime Time Productivity Program** is funded by the United States Department of Labor and by contributions from private employers. PTPP is a public/private partnership that works directly with employers in developing strategies for employing older workers. *Aging Workforce* is the publication offered by PTPP.

A resource manual has been developed by PTPP to assist service provider organizations in interfacing with private sector employers. Private employers will find information contained in the many helpful. Also included in the publication is an annotated bibliography.

AGING IN AMERICA
1500 Pelham Parkway
Bronx, New York 10461
Telephone: (212) 824-4004 (inside New York state)
           (800) 845-6900 (outside New York state)
Contact: Kathy Sisco, Director, Projects with Industry

Aging in America Inc./Projects with Industry is a private, nonprofit agency in nationwide partnerships with major corporations and small businesses to provide employers with skilled, experienced, mature employees.

Currently, thirty older worker satellites throughout the nation within the network can provide personnel or technical assistance for employers.

OLDER WOMEN'S LEAGUE (OWL)
730 Eleventh Street, N.W.
Suite 300
Washington, D.C. 20001
Telephone: (202) 783-6686
Contact: Joan A. Kuriansky, Executive Director

OWL is the first grass-roots membership organization to focus exclusively on the concerns of mid-life and older women. As a national advocacy organization, OWL works for policy changes to reduce inequities faced by older women. There are now 110 chapters across the country, with more than twenty thousand members and contributors. *The OWL Observer* is the national newspaper of the Older Women's League.

ALLIANCE FOR AGING RESEARCH
2021 K Street, N.W.
Suite 305
Washington, D.C. 20006
Telephone: (202) 293-2856
Contact: Daniel Perry, Executive Director

The Alliance for Aging Research is a private, nonprofit, tax-exempt organization that links the scientific community in human aging more closely with corporation and foundation executives and with Congress to promote aging research in the national interest. Alliance serves as a source of expertise to Congress and the executive branch on front-line research and private sector initiatives, including corporate practices aimed at rehiring and retaining older workers.

NATIONAL COMMISSION FOR EMPLOYMENT POLICY
1522 K Street, N.W., Suite 300
Washington, D.C. 20005
Publication: *Older Workers: Prospects, Problems, and Policies* (available free)

NATIONAL COMMISSION ON WORKING WOMEN OF WIDER OPPORTUNITIES FOR WOMEN
1325 G Street, N.W., Lower Level
Washington, D.C. 20005
Telephone: (202) 638-3143
Publication: *Women, Work and Age: A Report on Older Women and Employment* ($10; also available is a fact sheet for $1)

THE INSTITUTE ON AGING
Columbia University
622 W. 113th Street
New York, NY 10025
Telephone: (212) 854-4158
Publication: *Does America Need Older Workers?* ($6.95, including shipping and handling)

EQUAL EMPLOYMENT OPPORTUNITY COMMISSION
1801 L Street, N.W.
Washington, D.C. 20507
Telephone: 1-800-USA-EEOC

NATIONAL INDIAN COUNCIL ON AGING INC.
P.O. Box 2088
Albuquerque, New Mexico 87103
Telephone: (505) 242-9505
Contact: Curtis D. Cook, Executive Director

The National Indian Council on Aging Inc. operates a Seniors in Community Service Employment Program.

NATIONAL PACIFIC/ASIAN RESOURCE CENTER ON AGING
United Airlines Building
2033 Sixth Avenue, Suite 410
Seattle, Washington 98121
Telephone: (206) 448-0313
Contact: Louise M. Kamikawa, Executive Director

The National Pacific/Asian Resource Center on Aging operates a Seniors in Community Service Employment Program.

NATIONAL ASSOCIATION FOR HISPANIC ELDERLY
3225 Wilshire Blvd., 8th Floor
Los Angeles, California 90010
Telephone: (213) 487-1922
Contact: Carmela Lacayo

The National Association for Hispanic Elderly operates a Seniors in Community Service Employment Program.

CENTER FOR UNDERSTANDING AGING (CUA)
Framingham State College
Framingham, Massachusetts 01701
Telephone: (508) 626-4979
Contact: Fran Pratt, Executive Director

CUA is a nonprofit corporation formed in 1983 to educate the public about aging and to foster cross-generational understanding and cooperation. CUA specializes in helping other organizations develop or expand their own programs of aging education and intergenerational activity. Services include presentations and workshops, consultation and technical assistance, publications, information and referral, and a resource center.

AMERICAN SOCIETY ON AGING
833 Market Street
Suite 512
San Francisco, California 94103
Telephone: (415) 543-2617

ASA was founded in 1954 as the Western Gerontological Society, and works to promote the well-being of aging individuals and their families. ASA offers members an affiliation with the Business Forum on Aging, which addresses such issues as human resources, marketing, and consumer affairs. The Forum offers special programming, a quarterly newsletter, periodic "white papers" on selected topics, and an information clearinghouse.

ASA publishes a quarterly journal called *Generations*, as well as a bi-monthly newspaper, *The Aging Connection*.

FAMILIES USA FOUNDATION (Formerly, The Villers Foundation)
1334 G Street, N.W.
Washington, D.C. 20005
Telephone: (202) 628-3030
Contact: Cynthia B. Costello, Director, Employment and Volunteerism Policy

U.S. SENATE
SPECIAL COMMITTEE ON AGING
Room G-3, DSOB
Washington, D.C. 20510

GREEN THUMB, INC.
2000 N. 14th Street, Suite 800
Arlington, Virginia 22201
Telephone: (703) 522-7272
Contact: Andrea Wooten, President

Green Thumb, Inc. is a nonprofit corporation that operates in forty-four states and Puerto Rico as a job training and employment program for older Americans. Most of the participants in the Green Thumb program live in rural or suburban areas. Green Thumb operates a Seniors in Community Service Employment Program.

DIVISION OF OLDER WORKER PROGRAMS
Office of Special Targeted Programs
U.S. Department of Labor
Employment and Training Administration
Room N-4643
200 Constitution Ave., N.W.
Washington, D.C. 20210
Telephone: (202) 535-0521
Contact: Wilbert Solomon, Chief

DISPLACED HOMEMAKERS NETWORK
1411 K Street, N.W., Suite 930
Washington, D.C. 20005
Telephone: (202) 628-6767
Contact: Jill Miller, Executive Director

NATIONAL COUNCIL OF SENIOR CITIZENS
925 15th Street, N.W.
Washington, D.C. 20005
Telephone: (292) 347-8800
Contact: L.M. Wright, Acting Director, Senior Aides
Program

The National Council of Senior Citizens operates a Senior Aides Program, which is a Seniors in Community Service Employment Program.

NATIONAL CAUCUS AND CENTER ON BLACK AGED, INC.
1424 K Street, N.W.
Suite 500
Washington, D.C. 20005
Telephone: (202) 637-8400
Contact: Larry Crecy, V.P. Employment and Training, SCSEP Director

The National Caucus and Center on Black Aged, Inc. operates a Seniors in Community Service Employment Program.

NATIONAL ASSOCIATION OF STATE UNITS ON AGING (NASUA)
2033 K Street, N.W.
Suite 304
Washington, D.C. 20006
Telephone: (202) 785-0707
Contact: Ann Lordeman, Director, The National Clearinghouse on State and Local Older Worker Programs

A State Unit on Aging is an agency of state government designated by the governor and state legislature to be the focal point in the state for all matters concerning older citizens. *State Unit on Aging* is a generic term—the specific title and location in each state varies. The state unit can be a commission, an office, a department, a bureau, a council, or a board.

The National Clearinghouse on State and Local Older Worker Programs acts as a broker of information, making referrals to resources that can assist with specific issues. The Clearinghouse can put employers in touch with those people and resources that can help. NASUA also holds a conference, and will host its fifth conference in 1990.

State Units on Aging

Alabama
COMMISSION ON AGING
Oscar D. Tucker, Executive Director
Second Floor 136 Catoma Street
Montgomery, Alabama 36130
(205) 242-5743

Alaska
OLDER ALASKANS COMMISSION
Constance Sipe, Director
Department of Administration
Pouch C-Mail Station 0209
Juneau, Alaska 99811-0209
(907) 465-3250

Arizona
AGING AND ADULT ADMINISTRATION
Richard Littler, Director
Department of Economic Security
1400 West Washington Street
Phoenix, Arizona 85007
(602) 542-4446

Arkansas
DIVISION OF AGING AND ADULT SERVICES
Herb Sanderson, Director
Arkansas Department of Human Services
Donaghey Building, Suite 1417
7th and Main Streets
Little Rock, Arkansas 72201
(501) 682-2441

California
DEPARTMENT OF AGING
Alice Gonzales, Director
1600 K Street
Sacramento, California 95814
(916) 322-5290

Colorado
AGING AND ADULT SERVICE
Rita Barreras, Manager
Department of Social Services
1575 Sherman Street, 10th Floor
Denver, Colorado 80203-1714
(303) 866-3851

Connecticut
DEPARTMENT ON AGING
Mary Ellen Klinck, Commissioner
175 Main Street
Hartford, Connecticut 06106
(203) 566-3238

Delaware
DIVISION ON AGING
Eleanor Cain, Director
Department of Health and Social Services
1901 North DuPont Highway
New Castle, Delaware 19720
(302) 421-6791

District of Columbia
OFFICE ON AGING
Veronica Pace, Executive Director
1424 K Street, N.W.
2nd Floor
Washington, D.C. 20005
(202) 724-5626

Florida
PROGRAM OFFICE OF AGING
AND ADULT SERVICES
Larry Polivka, Assistant Secretary
Department of Health and Rehabilitation Services
1317 Winewood Boulevard
Tallahassee, Florida 32301
(904) 488-8922

Georgia
OFFICE OF AGING
Fred McGinnis, Director
878 Peachtree Street, N.E.
Room 632
Atlanta, Georgia 30309
(404) 894-5333

Guam
DIVISION OF SENIOR CITIZENS
Florence P. Shimizu, Administrator
Department of Public Health and Social Services
Government of Guam
P.O. Box 2816
Agana, Guam 96910

Hawaii
EXECUTIVE OFFICE ON AGING
Jeanette Takamura, Director
Office of the Governor
335 Merchant Street
Room 241
Honolulu, Hawaii 96813
(808) 548-2593

Idaho
OFFICE ON AGING
Charlene Martindale, Director
Room 114—Statehouse
Boise, Idaho 83720
(208) 334-3833

Illinois
DEPARTMENT ON AGING
Janet S. Otwell, Director
421 East Capitol Avenue
Springfield, Illinois 62701
(217) 785-2870

Indiana
DIVISION OF AGING SERVICES
George Brown, Director
Department of Human Services
251 North Illinois Street
P.O. Box 7083
Indianapolis, Indiana 46207-7083
(317) 232-7020

Iowa
DEPARTMENT OF ELDER AFFAIRS
Betty Grandquist, Executive Director
Suite 236, Jewett Building
914 Grand Avenue
Des Moines, Iowa 50319
(515) 281-5187

Kansas
DEPARTMENT ON AGING
Esther Valladolid Wolf, Secretary
915 S.W. Harrison
Topeka, Kansas 66612-1500
(913) 296-4986

Kentucky
DIVISION OF AGING SERVICES
Sue Tuttle, Director
Cabinet for Human Resources
CHR Building—6th West
275 East Main Street
Frankfort, KY 40621
(502) 564-6930

Louisiana
OFFICE OF ELDERLY AFFAIRS
Vickey Hunt, Director
P.O. Box 80374
Baton Rouge, Louisiana 70898
(504) 925-1700

Maine
BUREAU OF ELDER & ADULT SERVICES
Christine Gianopoulos, Director
Department of Human Services
State House—Station #11
Augusta, Maine 04333
(207) 289-2561

Maryland
OFFICE ON AGING
Rosalie Abrams, Director
State Office Building
301 West Preston Street, Rm. 1004
Baltimore, Maryland 21201
(301) 225-1100

Massachusetts
EXECUTIVE OFFICE OF ELDER AFFAIRS
Paul J. Lanzikos, Secretary
38 Chauncy Street
Boston, Massachusetts 02111
(617) 727-7750

Michigan
OFFICE OF SERVICES TO THE AGING
Olivia Maynard, Director
P.O. Box 30026
Lansing, Michigan 48909
(517) 373-8230

Minnesota
BOARD ON AGING
Gerald Bloedow
4th Floor, Human Services Bldg.
444 Lafayette Road
St. Paul, Minnesota 55155-3843
(612) 296-2770

Mississippi
COUNCIL ON AGING
Billie Marshall, Interim Director
Division of Aging and Adult Services
421 West Pascagoula Street
Jackson, Mississippi 39203
(601) 949-2070

Missouri
DIVISION ON AGING
Edwin Walker, Director
Department of Social Services
P.O. Box 1337
2701 W. Main St.
Jefferson City, Missouri 65102
(314) 751-3082

Montana
DEPARTMENT OF FAMILY SERVICES
Eugene Huntington, Director
48 North Last Chance Gulch
P.O. Box 8005
Helena, Montana 59604
(406) 444-5900

Nebraska
DEPARTMENT ON AGING
Betsy Palmer, Director
P.O. 95044
Lincoln, Nebraska 68509
(402) 471-2306

Nevada
DIVISION FOR AGING SERVICES
Suzanne Ernst, Administrator
Department of Human Resources
340 North 11th Street
Las Vegas, Nevada 89101
(702) 486-3545

New Hampshire
DIVISION OF ELDERLY AND ADULT SERVICES
Richard Chevrefils, Director
6 Hazen Drive
Concord, New Hampshire 03301-6501
(603) 271-4680

New Jersey
DIVISION ON AGING
Ann Zahora, Director
Department of Community Affairs
CN807
South Broad and Front Streets
Trenton, New Jersey 08625-0807
(609) 292-4833

New Mexico
STATE AGENCY ON AGING
Stephanie FallCreek, Director
224 East Palace Avenue, 4th Floor
La Villa Rivera Building
Santa Fe, New Mexico 87501
(505) 827-7640

New York
OFFICE FOR THE AGING
Jane Gould, Director
New York State Plaza
Agency Building #2
Albany, New York 12223
(518) 474-4425

North Carolina
DIVISION OF AGING
Alfred B. Boyles, Assistant Secretary
1985 Umstead Dr. Kirby Bldg.
Raleigh, North Carolina 27603
(919) 733-3983

North Dakota
AGING SERVICES
Larry Brewster, Administrator
Department of Human Services
State Capitol Building
Bismark, North Dakota 58505
(701) 224-2577

North Mariana Islands
OFFICE OF AGING
Edward Cabrera, Administrator
Department of Community and Cultural Affairs
Civic Center—Susupe
Saipan, Northern Mariana Island 96950

Ohio
DEPARTMENT OF AGING
Carol Austin, Director
50 West Broad Street, 9th Floor
Columbus, Ohio 43266-0501
(614) 466-5500

Oklahoma
AGING SERVICES DIVISION
Roy Keen, Division Administrator
Department of Human Services
P.O. Box 25352
Oklahoma City, Oklahoma 73125
(405) 521-2281

Oregon
SENIOR SERVICES DIVISION
Richard Ladd, Administrator
313 Public Service Building
Salem, Oregon 97310
(503) 378-4728

Pennsylvania
DEPARTMENT OF AGING
Linda Rhodes, Secretary
231 State Street
Harrisburg, Pennsylvania 17101-1195
(717) 783-1550

Puerto Rico
GERICULTURE COMMISSION
Celia E. Cintron, Executive Director
Department of Social Services
Apartado 11398
Santurce, Puerto Rico 00910
(809) 721-4010

Rhode Island
DEPARTMENT OF ELDERLY AFFAIRS
Adelaide Luber, Director
160 Pine Street
Providence, Rhode Island 02903-3708
(401) 277-2858

(American) Samoa
TERRITORIAL ADMINISTRATION ON AGING
Sunuitao Tupai, Director
Office of the Governor
Pago Pago, American Samoa 96799
011-684-633-1252

South Carolina
COMMISSION ON AGING
Ruth Seigler, Director
400 Arbor Lake Drive
Columbia, South Caroline 29223
(803) 735-0210

South Dakota
OFFICE OF ADULT SERVICES AND AGING
Gail Ferris, Executive Director
700 North Illinois Street
Kneip Building
Pierre, South Dakota 57501
(605) 773-3656

Tennessee
COMMISSION ON AGING
Emily Wiseman, Executive Director
Suite 201
Nashville, Tennessee 37219-5573
(615) 741-2056

Texas
DEPARTMENT ON AGING
O.P. (Bob) Bobbitt, Director
P.O. Box 12786 Capitol Station
1949 1H 35, South
Austin, Texas 78741-3702
(512) 444-2727

Federated States of Micronesia
FEDERATED STATES OF MICRONESIA
Wehns K. Billen, Director
Department of Human Resources
Kolonia, Pohnpei FM 96941
(691) 320-2733

Utah
DIVISION OF AGING AND ADULT SERVICES
Percy Devine, III, Director
Department of Social Services
120 North—200 West
Box 45500
Salt Lake City, Utah 84145-0500
(801) 538-3910

Vermont
DEPARTMENT OF REHABILITATION & AGING
Joel Cook, Commissioner
103 South Main Street
Waterbury, Vermont 05676
(802) 241-2400

Virginia
DEPARTMENT FOR THE AGING
Thelma Bland, Acting Commissioner
700 Centre, 10th Floor
700 East Franklin Street
Richmond, Virginia 23219-2327
(804) 225-2271

Virgin Islands
SENIOR CITIZEN AFFAIRS
Bernice Hall, Administrator
Department of Human Services

#19 Estate Diamond Fredericksted
St. Croix, Virgin Islands 00840
(809) 772-4950 ext. 46

Washington
AGING AND ADULT SERVICES ADMINISTRATION
Charles Reed, Assistant Secretary
Department of Social and Health Services
OB-44A
Olympia, Washington 98504
(206) 586-3768

West Virginia
COMMISSION ON AGING
David K. Brown, Executive Director
Holly Grove—State Capitol
Charleston, West Virginia 25305
(304) 348-3317

Wisconsin
BUREAU OF AGING
Donna McDowell, Director
Division of Community Services
217 South Hamilton Street, Suite 300
Madison, Wisconsin 53707
(608) 266-2536

Wyoming
COMMISSION ON AGING
Scott Sessions, Director
Hathaway Building—Room 139
Cheyenne, Wyoming 82002-0710
(307) 777-7986

Index

Ability is Ageless job fair, 88
Absenteeism, reduction by flextime, 155
Adult learning, 101–103
Accident rates for older workers, 40
Advertising for older workers, 58–67, 74–75, 80–85, 88
Age discrimination, xiv, 7, 21, 24, 61, 66, 69, 92–93, 124–125, 148, 176–183, 211; avoiding, 179–181; inadvertent, 179–181; legal action, 177–178
Age Discrimination in Employment Act, 30, 176–180
Age statistics, 1–9
Ageism, 176–183
Aging in America, 222
Alaska, 136
Alcohol consumption, 16–17
Alliance for Aging Research, 4
Amalgamated Life Insurance Company of New York, 141
American Association of Retired Persons, 208, 219–220; Worker Equity Department, 115
American Express, 134
American Society for Personnel Administration, 9, 20, 172
Andy Frain Communications, 203
Aptitude tests, 113
Assessment of older adults, 112
Authority in workplace, 151

Baby boom, 4
Baby bust, 7–9, 97

Bankers Life and Casualty, 202
Best Western Hotels, 204
Birthrate, 8
Builders Emporium, 203
Busch Gardens, 86
Business: keeping older workers, 7; recommendations for utilization of older workers, 21–26, 201–215; response to the aging workplace, 20–26

Career: burnout, 115; growth in older workers, 35; management, 170–176; obsolescence, 115–116; planning, 113, 171; plateauing, 115–116
Careers, dual, 4–5
Challenger, Gray & Christmas, Inc., 34
Champion International, 135
Chrysler Corporation, 141
Collins, Joan, 15
Commerce Clearing House, 20, 172
Commercials, depiction of older persons on, 15
Commission on Employment and Human Resources (Hawaii), 114
Communication, employee to employer, 184–185
Community resources for retirement planning, 192, 194
Community task forces for employment of older workers, 207, 209
Compensation, 11, 24, 60

Computer training, 109–111
Consultants, 164
Consumer preferences, 16–17
Contract work, 164
Control Data Corporation, 157, 167, 202
Corporate downsizing, 7
Corporate Retirees Network, 195–196

Data Products Corporation, 194
Days Inn, 86, 88
Defined benefit pension plans, 138
Defined contribution pension plans, 138
Demographic statistics, 1–9, 41–45
Direct mail for older worker recruitment, 83
Disney World, 59
Discrimination by age, xiv, 7, 21, 24, 61, 66, 69, 92–93, 124, 148, 176–183; avoiding, 179–181
Diversity of older workers, 23
Dual careers, 4–5
Dychtwald, Ken, 3

Early retirement, 138–139
Education, 16–17
Elder Care Solutions, 134
Eldercare by employees, 132–137
"Elderly," 30
Employee Assistance Programs, 134
Employee Benefit Research Institute, 136, 140
Employee communications, 213
Employee leasing, 165–166
Employee-to-employer communication, 184–185
Employer Challenge Initiative, 207
Employers: benefit costs of older workers, 38–39; perception of older workers, 19; as providers of Social Security information, 142–143; recommendations for utilization of older workers, 21–26; response to the aging workplace, 20–26; retention of older workers, 7
Employment: benefits, 60;

compensation, 60; of older workers, 201–215; part-time, 24–26, 53, 69; policy toward older workers, 21; selection of benefits by older workers, 128; status of older workers, 46–49
Entry-level jobs, 9

Financial Accounting Standards Board, 140
Flexible work schedules, 154–168
Flextime, 155–157
Franklin, Benjamin, 215

Geromarket, 15, 22
Goldring and Co., 15
Good People (agency), 203
Government-funded programs, 75–78, 120, 170
Grumman Corp., 1, 202

Hardee's Food Systems, 32, 62–65, 118–120, 126–127, 203
Health: education, 131–132; insurance, 129–130; screening, 131
Hearing, 104, 106
High technology, 105; teaching skills, 109–111
Hiring older workers, 92–93
Home, work at, 166
Honeywell Corporation, 135, 205–206
Human resources department, 181

Illiteracy, 97
Institute of Gerontology, 38
Insurance for long-term care, 133–137
International Foundation of Employee Benefit Plans, 133
Interviews, recruiting, 72

Japan, 4
Jargon, 107
Job: bank of older workers, 158–159; fairs, 87–88; flexibility, 212; orientation of older workers, 99; redesign for older workers,

117, 168–70, 212; sharing,
   159–161; stagnation, 115
Job Physical Assessment Tool, 114
Job Training Partnership Act, 76,
   120, 210
Jobs, physical requirements of, 114
Joseph Horn Department Store, 203

Kelly Services, 126, 163, 203, 205
Kentucky Fried Chicken, xiv, 32, 86,
   118, 203, 215
Kollmorgen Corporation, 193

Labor force, aging of, 2–5
Labor force participation, 6
Labor: cost, 11–12; market
   conditions, 22; quality, 10–11;
   shortage, 7–12, 20–22, 158;
   turnover, 11
Labor policy toward older workers,
   21
Learning, adult, 101–103; self-paced,
   105; speed of, 104–105
Leasing of employees, 165–166
Legal action for age discrimination,
   177–178
Life expectancy, increase of, 5
Life experience, pay for, 125
Lifestyles of older people, 49–54;
   diversity of, 52–53
Lifetime employment, 14
Long-term care, 132–137; insurance
   for, 133–137

Magazines for senior market, 18
Maitlen, B.R., and Associates,
   197–199
Management of older workers,
   147–186
Management styles, authoritative vs.
   participative, 153
Management support for
   older-worker programs, 210–211
Management training programs for
   older workers, 118
Marketing to older consumer, 15–19
Mass-transit advertising, 84
Massey, Morris, 32–34
McDonald's, 1, 32, 118

Medical benefits, postretirement, 140
Medicare, 140–142; administration
   by employees, 141
Medicare Insured Groups, 141
Mercer-Meidinger-Hansen, 136, 142
Mexico, 4
Misconceptions of older persons,
   18–19, 23, 119
Motivating the problem older
   employee, 174

National Alliance of Business, 21
National Association for Senior
   Living Industries, 50
National Council on the Aging, 192,
   208, 221–222
National Institute on Aging, 5
National Staff Leasing Association,
   165
National Urban League, 208, 220
New Jersey Older Worker Task
   Force, 207
New York City Department of
   Aging, 88
Newton & Associates, 47, 69, 99

Occupations of older workers, 46
Older Americans Act, 120
Older consumer, 15–19
Older persons: acceptable labels for,
   182; accomplishments of,
   215–216; assessment of, 111–114;
   diversity of, 49–54; education of,
   51–52; employment status, 46–49;
   hearing of, 104, 106; inadequacy
   of retirement income, 36; income,
   51–52; introversion, 50–51;
   learning speed of, 104–105;
   lifestyles of, 49–54; perceptions
   of, 14–15, 18–19; poverty, 44;
   preference for work vs. retirement,
   48; reentry into work force, 79;
   self-reliance of, 50–51; technology
   training, 109–111; training of,
   103, 106–109; unfamiliarity with
   high technology, 105; values of,
   49–54; vision of, 104–106
Older Persons with Active Lifestyles
   (OPALS), 15

Older Women's League, 15, 222–223
Older workers: accident rates, 40;
  advertising for, 58–67, 80–85;
  barriers to job performance, 168;
  benefit costs, 38–39; career
  growth, 35; compensation of, 24,
  124–125; definition, 29–31;
  demographics, 41–45; employment
  of, 201–215; employment policies,
  21; female, 44–45; flexibility, 35;
  grievance resolution, 184; health
  insurance, 129–130; intelligence,
  41; job orientatlon, 99; job
  performance of, 149, 172–174,
  181, 184; job redesign for, 117,
  168–170, 204–206; job tenure,
  34; labels, 31; learning ability, 38;
  managing, 170–176, 184–185;
  management support for,
  210–211; management training
  for, 118; motivating, 174–175;
  myths, 31–42, 119; occupations
  of, 46; perceptions of, 19, 23,
  31–42, 119; physical capabilities
  of, 113–114; productivity, 33;
  profile of, 29–53;
  recommendations for utilization,
  21–26; recruitment of, 23, 48,
  52–54, 57–93, 204–205, 207;
  reentry from retirement, 39;
  regularity of attendance, 36;
  relationships with coworkers, 37;
  rescheduling woik for, 169;
  resources concerning, 206–209;
  retention by businesses, 7, 13, 98,
  147–186; retraining of, 97–121;
  screening, 92; seeking out in
  recruiting, 73; self-confidence, lack
  of, 113; stereotypes of, 32, 148;
  stress of new job, 99; and
  temporary help agencies, 162;
  training of, 23, 97–121; utilization
  of, 208–214; work ethic, 34;
  workforce participation rates,
  43–44; values of, in contrast with
  younger workers, 150–153
Older Workers League, 206
On-the-job training, 100
Open houses for recruiting, 82–83

Operation Able, 84, 207
Orientation of older workers, 99
Ostroff, Jeff, 18

Part-time employment, 24–26, 53,
  69, 91, 139, 149–150, 157–159
Pay rates for older workers, 124–125
Peller, Clara, 15
Pensions, 137–139; defined
  benefit/contribution plans, 138
Pepsico, 135
Performance appraisal for older
  workers, 173–174, 181
Physical capabilities of older workers,
  113–114
Physical requirements for jobs, 114
Polaroid Corporation, 194
Population, aging of, 3–6
Postretirement medical benefits, 140
Poverty, 44
Preretirement planning, 197–199
Pretraining, 100–101
Private Industry Councils, 76, 109,
  120, 210
Proctor & Gamble, 134
Productivity, increase by flextime,
  155
Promotions, 151
Psychographic analysis, 50–52, 66

Quality of labor, 10

Radio advertising, 88
Recruiting: activities, 68; advertising,
  58–67, 74–75; difficulties, 9–12;
  help from organizations, 76–79;
  interviews, 72; job fairs, 87–88;
  market, 57; messages, 66–71; of
  older workers, 23, 48, 52–54, 73,
  204–205, 207; open houses,
  82–83; referrals, 85; screening,
  92; strategies, 57–91; targeting
  older workers, 61, 212; task
  forces, 86; telemarketing, 89; vans,
  89–90
Redesigning work for older workers,
  204–206
Retention of older workers, 98;
  147–186

Retiree job bank, 159–159
Retiree Skills Inc. 203
Retirement, 5–7, 46–49, 70;
  assistance after, 196; community
  resources for planning, 192, 194;
  early, 138–139, 190; forced, 7,
  215; gradual, 149–150;
  inadequacy of income, 36, 191;
  networks, 196; policies, 24–26;
  planning, 191–199; preference vs.
  working, 48; reentry from, 39, 47,
  90–91; rehearsing, 193; statistics,
  189; unfunded commitments, 140;
  unhappiness with, 190–191; work
  options in, 198
Retraining older workers, 97–121

Sanders, Col. Harland, xiv, 215–217
Scheduling adaptation for older
  workers, 169
Self-paced learning, 105
Seminars, 83
"Senior citizens," 30
Senior Communications Services, 101
Senior Community Service
  Employment Program, 76
Senior Employment Resources, 101
Senior Power (agency), 163, 203
Shenandoah Life Insurance, 13–14
Skills inventories, 112–113
Skill upgrading, 116–117
Social Security, 217; benefits, 40, 45,
  137–138; information from
  employers, 142; reduction of
  benefits due to earnings, 125–128
Society for Human Resources
  Management, 9, 20, 172
Stagnation on job, 115
State departments on aging, 229–241
Stereotypes of older workers, 148
Supervisor training relative to older
  workers, 213
Support services for employment of
  older workers, 206–207

Tardiness, reduction by flextime,
  157
Task forces for recruiting, 86
Task forces of older workers, 213

Tax-deferred dependent care accounts,
  135
Teaching high-technology skills,
  109–111
Technological change, 97
Tecnnology training for older adults,
  109–111
Telecommuting, 166
Telemarketing, 89
Television advertising, 83
Television stars, older, 15
Temporary employment, 161–163
Temporary help agencies, 162
Texas Refinery Corporation, 159
Thompson, J. Walter (advertising
  agency), 15
Training older workers, 23, 97–121;
  classes, 109–111; methodologies
  for, 106–109
Travelers, The, 1, 109, 132,
  135–136, 158–159, 196

Unemployment, 46–49
Unfunded retirement commitments,
  140
United States: Administration on
  Aging, 30; Bureau of the Census,
  4
University of Michigan Institute for
  Social Research, 33
University of Southern California, 5

Values of older people, 49–54;
  diversity, 52–53
Values of older vs younger workers,
  150–153
Vans, recruiting, 89–90
Varian Associates, 90
Vision, 104–106

Wal-Mart Stores, 203
Walt Disney World, 202
Washington Business Group on
  Health, 129–133
Wellness programs, 129–132, 193
Wells Fargo Bank, 1
Westinghouse, 179
Women as older workers, 44
Work at home, 166

Work, enjoyment of, 151
Work ethic, 34, 150–151
Work force: aging of, 1–5;
  participation rates, 43–44; reentry
  into, 79
Work options for retirees, 198

Work schedules, flexibile, 154–168
Workplace expectations, 171

Yankelovich, Skelly, and White, 32
Young workers, lack of skills in, 13

About the Author

Catherine D. Fyock, A.E.P., is president of Innovative Management Concepts, a consulting firm specializing in nontraditional solutions to employment issues. She works with businesses in developing creative solutions for finding and keeping top employees, and in particular, strategies for reaching nontraditional labor market segments, such as the older worker.

Her clients include Hardee's Food Systems, Hallmark Cards, Westin Hotels and Resorts, the National Council on the Aging, Inc., and the National Association of State Units on Aging.

Before founding her own consulting company, Fyock was Director of Human Resources for Kentucky Fried Chicken Corporation, where she developed the "Colonel's Tradition," a national initiative for employing the older worker.

Fyock, a noted lecturer and seminar leader, is a member of the Society for Human Resources Management, serving on its national committee for Training and Development. She is a member of the National Speakers Association, and is an officer of her chapter. She has a bachelor's degree from Western Kentucky University, a master's degree in Personnel Management from the University of Louisville, and is an Accredited Executive in Personnel.

For further information on services provided by Innovative Management Concepts, contact Catherine Fyock at P.O. Box 905, Prospect, Kentucky 40059, tel. (502) 228-3869.